Joseph Strutt

The Regal and Ecclesiastical Antiquities of England

Containing the representations of all the English monarchs, from Edward the Confessor to

Henry the Eighth, together with many of the great persons that were eminent under their

several reigns

Joseph Strutt

The Regal and Ecclesiastical Antiquities of England
Containing the representations of all the English monarchs, from Edward the Confessor to Henry the Eighth, together with many of the great persons that were eminent under their several reigns

ISBN/EAN: 9783743407138

Manufactured in Europe, USA, Canada, Australia, Japa

Cover: Foto ©ninafisch / pixelio.de

Manufactured and distributed by brebook publishing software (www.brebook.com)

Joseph Strutt

The Regal and Ecclesiastical Antiquities of England

THE

REGAL AND ECCLESIASTICAL

ANTIQUITIES OF ENGLAND:

CONTAINING

THE REPRESENTATIONS OF ALL THE ENGLISH MONARCHS,

FROM

EDWARD THE CONFESSOR TO HENRY THE EIGHTH;

TOGETHER WITH

Many of the Great Perfons that were eminent under their feveral Reigns;

ON SIXTY COPPER PLATES, ENGRAVED BY THE AUTHOR.

THE WHOLE

CAREFULLY COLLECTED FROM ANCIENT ILLUMINATED MANUSCRIPTS.

By *JOSEPH STRUTT.*

A NEW EDITION,

TO WHICH IS NOW ADDED A SUPPLEMENT, CONTAINING TWELVE PLATES.

LONDON:
PRINTED FOR BENJAMIN AND JOHN WHITE, FLEET-STREET.

1793.

TO THE READER.

THE work now offered to the public will (the author hopes) prove in some measure useful to the artists, as well as pleasing to the curious:—useful, because those who have occasion to represent scenes from the English history, may find the dress and character of the ancient times; —and pleasing to the curious, because these pictures are the most likely to contain the exact representation of the customs and manners of the earlier æra of our ancestors.

HITHERTO our artists have been extremely deficient in their delineations of the early history.—The Saxons are frequently drawn in the habit of the figures on the Trajan and Antonine columns; and the Normans are put into the dresses and armour worn in Edward the Fourth's time, and indeed are often made still more modern.

IT may be said, perhaps, in the defence of the artist, that models, sufficiently authentic for his purpose, are very much wanted.—Our monuments, and statues, are exceedingly difficult to ascertain; and, even of these, there are few of any note, of earlier date than Henry the Seventh. And our coins are still of less use, being so miserably executed as scarce to bear the resemblance of any thing.—From these imperfect lights, it was not possible for artists to come at the truth of antiquity, so that they were obliged to supply from their own fancy whatever they thought deficient; by which means errors were frequently made, even when corrections were intended.

FROM the statues and bas-reliefs of the Greeks and Romans, the character, dress and customs of those nations are become perfectly clear and intelligible to us; but with respect to the antiquities of this country the case is very different,

TO THE READER.

different, for there is scarcely any one able to determine the sort of habit worn in the time of Edward the First.

NEVERTHELESS, though we cannot come at such complete and excellent remains of our earlier time as are left by the Greeks and Romans, the author hopes that the following work (which contains the most ancient national materials that remain) will be thought capable of removing, in a considerable degree, the former obscurity, especially with respect to such circumstances as the dress and personal appearance of our monarchs.

FROM Edward the Confessor, the series is perfectly complete, and interspersed with various passages of history; so that it is not only a view of the kings of England, but a representation of part of their transactions, and the portraits of many of the great and remarkable personages living under their reign.—And the authority is undoubted, since the illuminations were made in, or soon after, the reign of each particular monarch.

As no work of this kind (viz. in a regular series) has been yet attempted in this kingdom, the author humbly hopes that the indulgent public will excuse whatever they may find amiss or defective; and he, on his part, begs leave to assure them, that he has done, and will always do, the utmost in his power to render the work a perfect copy of the valuable originals: and the more so, as many of the figures are undoubtedly actual portraits of the kings, &c. represented.

I.

REGAL AND ECCLESIASTICAL ANTIQUITIES, &c.

A DESCRIPTION OF THE PLATES.

No. I.

KING EDGAR.

THIS engraving is taken from a curious and ancient illumination found in a book of grants *, given by king Edgar himfelf to Winchefter Cathedral. It is dated A. D. 966, and is written entirely in letters of gold, in the old Saxon character.

Edgar is here delineated as piouſly adoring our bleſſed Saviour, who appears above feated on a globe, to fhew his empire, and fupported by four angels, emblems of the four goſpels; under his feet are two folding doors, intended perhaps to reprefent the entrance into the bottomlefs pit, which is fo placed to convey the idea of his triumph over Death and Hell; in his left hand he holds the book of judgment, which is to be opened in the laft day. The figure on the right hand of the king, I fancy, may be done for Cuthbert, the faint of Durham, whofe holy life is recorded by the venerable Bede. The woman, not unlikely, is the famous Etheldrida, abbefs of Ely, who, though fhe were twice married, yet lived and died a pure virgin.

We fhall not wonder at feeing Edgar, who was indeed a man of loofe character, reprefented as a particular favorite of Chrift and the departed faints, when we recollect that he did greater things for the clergy in general, and built more monafteries and religious houfes, than any of his predecef-

---

* The firft fifteen plates of this collection are taken from the illuminations of antient MSS. in the Cottonian library, at the Britifh Mufeum; and this book of grants is mark'd Vefpafianus, A. VIII.

fors;

fors; therefore the leaſt which the monks of that day could do, was to pay him this pleaſing compliment. For the ſame cauſe may thoſe two ſaints be portrayed beſide him, as being the moſt famous for their holineſs, and love of a monaſtic life, of any recorded in the Saxon annals. On the oppoſite page is written, in capital letters of gold,

Sic celyo peyrbet Solio qui conbibic Ayτρa,
Rex venepans Eabʒaη pponus aboηaτ eum.

"Thus fits that god alone, who made the heavens, whilſt humbly Edgar the king pays his adoration."

As there has been extraordinary pains taken in the writing and ornaments of this book, and as it was written (which appears by the date) in the very time of Edgar, it is more than barely probable that this is not only an exact delineation of the habit of that monarch, but alſo (to the beſt of the illuminator's power) a true portrait of him.

Becauſe ſome of the purchaſers may chooſe to amuſe themſelves in colouring of the plates, the author has carefully deſcribed the colours of the original.--- The garment of our Saviour is a dark blue, and the lighter robe is gold; ſo alſo is the oval he ſits in, the book he holds, and the doors under his feet. The angels are dreſſed in white, and the ſhadowed part is gold, as well on the habit as on the wings. The king's cloak is a dark blue, edged with gold; his coat a deepiſh crimſon, and his hoſe a dark brown; his book and crown are gold. The ſaints, on each ſide of him, are in blue, and the lighter coloured part of their garments is gold, as well as the ornaments they hold, and the glory over their heads.

TEN

ANTIQUITIES OF ENGLAND.

TEN of the following plates are taken from a curious MS.* written in the time of Edward the First, and illuminated with great care. The author has written a short account in old French of each illumination, under it, alternately in blue and gold letters. He has placed this short prelude over the first illumination:

Icy funt les Rops de Engleterre, del tens feput Edwazde le Confeffor, jesfie al tens le rop Edwazde fils Henrp le Tpers.

" Here are [portrayed] the kings of England, from the time of faint Edward the Confeffor, to the time of king Edward, the fon of Henry the Third."

No. II.

EDWARD THE CONFESSOR.

THE character of Edward the Confeffor is fufficiently known, and the title of faint, which was given to him, rather for the protection of the clergy, and his auftere conduct in the outward forms of religion, than his actual holinefs; for his behaviour as a king, as a hufband, and as a man, is often very exceptionable; and the caufelefs ill-treatment of his virtuous queen, Edgitha, who is here reprefented fitting at his right hand, is a conftant blot upon his character. His only excufe is, that fhe was the daughter of Goodwin, earl of Kent, a man who had rendered himfelf odious to the king. Yet furely the innocent ought not to fuffer for the guilty; but fuch was Edward's difpofition, that what he did not dare to revenge upon the father, he repayed to the daughter.

The ftory here reprefented, is an event of a moft extraordinary nature,— Edward, with his queen and Goodwin, are at a banquet which the king gave on Eafter day. Whilft they were at meat, the king accufed Goodwin of being acceffary to the murder of his brother, which he pofitively denied, folemnly wifhing that the morfel of meat which he then put into his mouth might fuddenly ftrangle him, if he was not perfectly innocent. This egregious untruth drew down upon him the juft judgment of God; for in attempting to fwallow the meat, he was really choaked, and fell down dead that very inftant.

* Vitellius, A. XIII.

The

The author gives this account of his picture:

Sepnt Cdwarde, par la grace Deu, vist le jour de paike al manger; les vii dormanz turner lur bestre cortez fur lur fenestre en gre. E cet jour Godwyne Conte de Bent morust a la table, estrangle de un morfel. Pult grant miracles fur den par lup en fa vie e apres.

Le an del incarnacion nostre Seignur M.LXVI. e de foen reaume xxiiii. devant fa mort devifa feput Edwarde le reaume de Engeltere a William Bastarde foen nevou a dunke de Normundye. E puis morust feput Edwarde, e gist enferer a Westmustre.

Which is in English as follows:

" As faint Edward (by the grace of God) was fitting at meat on Eafter day, the Seven Sleepers turned from their right fide to the left of their own accord. And that very day Goodwyne earl of Kent died at the table, ftrangled by a morfel of meat. Many great miracles did God work by him (that is king Edward) in his life-time and afterwards.

" The year of the incarnation of our Lord 1066, and of his reign the 24th, king Edward, before his death, gave the kingdom of England to William the Baftard, his nephew, at that time duke of Normandy. After this died faint Edward, and lies buried at Weftminfter."

The popular ftory of the Seven Sleepers is often alluded to in ancient books, but fo imperfectly, that all which I can gather concerning them is, that they were feven travellers, who being weary, laid themfelves down in a cave to fleep, and by fome fupernatural means they continued fleeping for an amazing fpace of time.

The ten illuminations copied from this MS. are very fimple in point of colouring, being fcarcely more than three, or four colours at moft. All the garments are either dark, or light browns; the crowns, fceptres, and other ornaments, are gold; the faces, linen, and infide of the cloaks, are expreffed by the vellum itfelf, flightly fhaded, and left clear for the lights. The light back grounds are gold; and the dark ones blue, with gold ftars.

No. III.

HAROLD AND WILLIAM THE CONQUEROR.

AFTER the death of Edward, Harold, notwithstanding his oath and engagements to be assisting in placing the duke of Normandy on the throne, caused himself to be crowned king. But he did not long enjoy the fruits of his perjury; for William, hearing of the death of the Confessor, came over into England with a great army, and landed at Hastings, where he was met by Harold, and a bloody battle ensued. But the end proved unfortunate to Harold and his party; for he being slain by an arrow which struck him in the eye, the field was lost, and the English were put to flight.

The present plate represents that fatal action. On the right we see the Conqueror mounted on his horse, trapped with his arms; whilst, on the other side, the unfortunate Harold is falling from his horse, having just received his death's wound. The illuminator, who lived in the reign of Edward the First, has not attended to the dress and customs of the times which he means to represent; for the armour, cross bows, banners, &c. which are delineated in this piece, were used in the æra in which he lived, but not at the time of the Conquest.

This important battle was fought about nine miles from Hastings, in Sussex, upon the 14th day of October, being Saturday, the year of our Lord 1066.

Take the following homely verses from Stow, on this occasion:

> A thousand six and sixty years
> It was, as we do read,
> When that a comet did appear,
> And Englishmen lay dead;
> Of Normandy duke William, then
> To England ward did sail,
> Who conquered Harold with his men,
> And brought the land to bayle.

REGAL AND ECCLESIASTICAL

Under Harold is written,

𝔄𝔭𝔯𝔢𝔰 𝔠𝔢𝔭𝔲𝔱 𝔈𝔡𝔴𝔞𝔯𝔡𝔢 𝔯𝔢𝔤𝔫𝔞 𝔥𝔞𝔯𝔞𝔩𝔡, 𝔩𝔢 𝔣𝔦𝔷 𝔊𝔬𝔡𝔢𝔴𝔶𝔫 𝔠𝔬𝔲𝔫𝔱 𝔡𝔢 𝔎𝔢𝔫𝔱. 𝔄 𝔣𝔬𝔯𝔷 𝔢𝔫 𝔱𝔬𝔯𝔱 𝔦𝔵 𝔪𝔬𝔭𝔰. 𝔇𝔲𝔫𝔨𝔢 𝔳𝔢𝔫𝔱 𝔚𝔦𝔩𝔩. 𝔅𝔞𝔰𝔱𝔞𝔯𝔡𝔢, 𝔢 𝔩𝔢 𝔱𝔬𝔩𝔲𝔰𝔱 𝔩𝔞 𝔳𝔶𝔢, 𝔢 𝔩𝔢 𝔯𝔢𝔤𝔫𝔢, 𝔢 𝔠𝔬𝔫𝔮𝔲𝔦𝔰𝔱 𝔩𝔞 𝔱𝔢𝔯𝔢.—𝔥𝔞𝔯𝔞𝔩𝔡𝔢 𝔤𝔦𝔰𝔱 𝔞 𝔚𝔞𝔩𝔱𝔥𝔞𝔪𝔢.

Which may be thus tranflated:

" After faint Edward reigned Harold, the fon of Goodwyn earl of Kent, for the fpace of nine months, when William the Baftard came [into England] and deprived him at once of his life and the kingdom, and conquered the land. Harold lies [buried] at Walthàm."

Under William is written,

𝔓𝔲𝔦𝔰 𝔯𝔢𝔤𝔫𝔞 𝔚𝔦𝔩𝔩. 𝔅𝔞𝔰𝔱𝔞𝔯𝔡𝔢 𝔵𝔵 𝔞𝔫, 𝔭𝔲𝔦𝔰 𝔪𝔬𝔯𝔲𝔰𝔱, 𝔢 𝔤𝔦𝔰𝔱 𝔞 𝔎𝔞𝔫𝔢 𝔢𝔫 𝔑𝔬𝔯𝔪𝔲𝔫𝔡𝔶𝔢.

" After him reigned William the Baftard twenty years, when he died, and lies [buried] at Caen in Normandy."

This illumination is found in the fame MS. with the former No. II. and the colours are there defcribed.

No. IV.

IV

No. IV.

WILLIAM RUFUS.

WILLIAM RUFUS was the second son of the Conqueror. The illuminator has here represented him in his robes of state.

Under this king is written,

Apres Will. Bastard regna Will, le Rous sun fiz. Il fust berge en la Nobele Forest. Puis moruft, egist a Wynceftre. Il fist fere la grande sale de Westmufter, e regna xii auns.

"After William the Bastard reigned William Rufus [or the Red] his son. He was slain in the New Forest. Being dead, he was buried at Winchester. He caused the great hall of Westminster to be made, and reigned twelve years."

King William (says Stow) on the morrowe after Lammas daye, hunting in the New Forrest of Hampshire, in a place called Chorengham, where since a chapel was builded, Sir Walter Tirell shooting at a deer, unawares hit the king in the breast, that he fell downe stark dead, and never spake word more. His men (especially that knight who had wounded him) gat away; but some came back again, and laid his body upon a colliar's cart, which one feelie leane beaste did drawe unto the city of Winchester, where he was buried on the morrow after his death. At whose burial men could not weep for joy.

Before we conclude with this prince, we will set before the reader the following anecdote concerning him, as given by the old poetic historian Robert of Glocefter, which plainly denotes his pride. The verses, divested of their obsolete orthography, run as follows:

> As his chamberlein him brought as he arose one day,
> The morrow for to wear, a pair of hose of sey,
> He ask'd what they cost him. Three shillings, the other said.
> Fy a dibles! quoth the king. Who says so vile a deed?
> A king wear any cloth, but what should cost much more;
> Buy a pair of a mark, or you shall rue it sore!

A worse

REGAL AND ECCLESIASTICAL

A worfe pair full enough the other fith him brought,
And faid they coft a mark, and therefore fo were bought.
A bel amy, quoth the king, thefe are now well bought;
In this manner ferve thou me, or thou fhalt ferve me not.'

This plate is from the fame MS. with the former, and coloured as defcribed page 4.

No. V.

HENRY THE FIRST,

Is also drawn in his robes of state, and of him the author says,

Apres Will. le Rous, regna la primer Henry, sun frere, xxxv. auns. Il fit les bones laps de Engleter, si les enchartera. Il gist a l'Abbaye de Redynges.—Son cors leva seynt Thomas de tere, e le mist devaunt le haut auter.

"After William Rufus, reigned the first Henry, his brother, thirty-five years. He made the good laws of England, which he caused to be enrolled. He lies buried at the Abbey of Reading.—His body was taken from the earth by saint Thomas, and placed before the high altar."

Henry the First was surnamed Beauclerc. This appellation was bestowed upon him for his learning (which was very uncommon in those days, except amongst the clergy). This prince mounted the throne the second day of August 1100, and was much beloved by his people. He made (according to the French author) the good laws of England; but the truth is, he abolished the hard and rigorous statutes which had been established by his father and brother, and restored those by much more equal, and suited to the tempers of the people, which were in force in the days of the Confessor.

The worst action of Henry was the cruel treatment of his brother Robert; for he not only caused him to be closely kept in prison, but, because he attempted to escape, deprived him of his eye-sight.—As the circumstances concerning the death of this Robert are rather extraordinary, they are here set down, as related by Holingshed.

"It is sayde that on a festival day king Henrie put on a robe of scarlet, the cape whereof being strayte, hee rente it in stryving to put it over hys heade; and perceyving it would not serve him, he layd it aside, and sayde, Let my brother Robert have this garment, who hath a sharper head than I have. The which, when it was brought to duke Robert, the rent place being not sewed up, he discovered it, and asked whether any man had worne it before. The messenger tolde the whole matter, how it happened. Herewith duke Robert tooke such a griefe for the scornefull mocke of his brother, that he waxed wearie of his life, and fayde, Nowe I perceyve I have lived too long, that my brother shall clothe me like his almes-man, with his cast rent garments. And thus cursing the time of his nativity, refused from thenceforth to eate or drink, and so pined away, and was buryed at Gloucester*."

This plate is from the same MS. and coloured as the former.

* Holing. Chron. Vol. 2, fol. 363.

VI

No. VI.

STEPHEN.

This king is here represented in the common robes usually worn by the nobility, and not in the robes of state. On his finger he carries a hawk; an emblem of his being nobly born, though not the immediate son of a king.—He was third son to Stephen earl of Blois, by Alice, fourth daughter of the Conqueror.

Of this prince the French author says,

Apres Henry, regna Esteven, son nevou, xix anse, e morust. E gist a Faversham.

"After Henry, reigned Stephen, his nephew, 19 years, and died. He lies [buried] at Feversham."

Stephen (says Stow) was a man of passing comely features and personage; he also excelled in martial policy, gentleness and liberality towards all men; and though his reign was disturbed by continual wars, yet did he never burden his commons with any heavy exactions: so that he only wanted a just title to the crown, to secure him the character of an excellent and worthy king.

His wars were chiefly against Matilda, the daughter of the deceased king Henry. She was married to the emperor Henry the Fourth, whom she survived, and after the death of her father came over into England, and being a woman of great courage, asserted boldly her right to the crown against Stephen, who, contrary to a solemn oath which he had taken, had ascended the throne himself.

The caprice of the people prevailed upon them to abandon Stephen, and attend to the cause of the injured Matilda; so that he lost a decisive battle, and was taken prisoner. But Matilda soon after discovered a tyrannical disposition, which was displeasing to the nobility; wherefore, rescuing Stephen from his confinement, they reinstated him in the throne, and Matilda, in her turn, experienced the sudden change of inconstant fortune. Flying from the forces of Stephen, she was driven to such straits, that to prevent her being discovered, she was conveyed through Glocester in a litter like a dead corpse; and, after shutting herself up in the castle of Oxford, which was girt round with a clofe fiege by her enemies, her dangerous fituation caufed her to put the following extraordinary fcheme in execution, in order to effect her efcape :—It being mid-winter, and the ground covered with fnow, fhe habited herfelf and fome few attendants in white garments, and in the middle of the nigh tfled filently out of an obfcure poftern: fhe paffed unfeen by her enemies; and, croffing the Thames, purfued her journey on foot to Wallingford, and from thence fome time after departed into Normandy.

His next troubles arofe from Henry, the fon of Matilda; but, after fome difcord, the matter was amicably fettled, and Henry ordained to inherit the crown, upon the death of Stephen.

No. VII.

HENRY THE SECOND.

HERE we have exhibited king Henry the Second in his coronation habit. The author thus writes of him:

Apres Esteven, regna le secund Henrp. fiz de la sorour Emperice; le quele Henrp lo:s estopt duke de Normundpe. En sun temps fu sepure Thomas ma:tprije. e regna xxvi ou xxxv auns. Puis morust, e gist a Fiunt Euajd.

"After Stephen, reigned the second Henry, son of the emprefs; which Henry was duke of Normandy. In his time was faint Thomas martyred. He reigned 26 or 35 years. After dying, he was buried at Front Euard."

According to the agreement made between Stephen and prince Henry, the fon of Matilda the emprefs, after the death of the former, Henry came into England, and was accordingly crowned king of England.

One of the moft remarkable anecdotes relative to this king, is his love to Rofamunda, the fair daughter of Walter lord Clifford; for whom (fays Stow) he made a houfe of wonderful working, fo that no perfon could come to her, unlefs he were inftructed by the king, or fuch as were acquainted with the fecret. This houfe, after feen, was named LABYRINTHUS, or DÆDALUS WORK, which was thought to be conftructed like unto a knot in a garden called a maze. It is faid that the queen, her profeffed enemy, gained admiffion by a clue of thread or filk, and either by poifon, or fome other fatal method, caufed her death. Henry was greatly affected with her lofs, and caufed her to be honourably interred at Godftow, near Oxford, in a houfe of nuns, and thefe verfes were put upon her tomb:

   Hic jacet in tumba, Rofa Mundi, non rofa munda
   Non redolet, fed olet, quæ redolere folet.

Which

Which we find in Fabian thus tranſlated, or rather paraphraſed:

> The roſe of the world, but not the cleane flowre,
> Is now here graven, to whom beaute was lent.
> In this grave full darke now is her bowre,
>   That by her life was ſweete and rodolent,
>   But now that ſhe is from this life bent,
> Though ſhe were ſweete, now foully doth ſhe ſtinke;
> A mirrour good for all men that on her thinke.

There is yet to be ſeen at Godſtow, the chapel where it is ſaid that ſhe was buried; and theſe verſes are wrote upon the wall in the inſide of the ſame.

This illumination is taken alſo from the ſame MS. as the former, and is coloured in like manner.

No. VIII.

No. VIII.[*]

HENRY THE SECOND AND THOMAS BECKET.

This illumination represents one of the most important passages of Henry's life,—the dispute between him and the proud prelate Thomas Becket, archbishop of Canterbury. The king, in his royal robes, is seated on his throne, and surrounded by his guard; before him stands Becket, attired in his pontifical habit, holding the cross in his hand. The arrogance of Becket is well expressed in this little delineation, as well in his face as his attitude; as is also the anger of the king.

The whole circumstance at large is as follows:

Whilst the dispute ran high between the king and Becket, " divers accusations (says Speed) were laid against him, as of contempt towards the king, in denying to come into his presence, being thereto commanded by him, and many other matters; whereto though he made excuses (reasonable enough, if true) yet the peers and bishops condemned all his moveables to the king's mercy: and the prelates, perceiving the king's displeasure to tend yet to some farther severity, premonished him to submit himself, for that otherwise the king's court intended to adjudge him a perjured person, and also a traytor, for not yielding temporal allegiance to his temporal sovereign, as himself had sworn to do; and accordingly the prelates themselves, by joint consent, adjudged him of perjury, and by the mouth of the bishop of Chichester, disclaimed thenceforward all obedience unto him as their archbishop. The next day, whilst the bishops and peers were consulting of some further course with him, Becket, not as yet daunted, caused to be sung before him at the altar this psalm:

" The princes sit and speak against me, and the ungodly persecute me, &c."

---

[*] This is from Claudius, D. 2. a MS. in the Cotton library. In the MS. there is a duplicate of this illumination; the subject is exactly the same; and the only difference is in the figure behind Becket, who bears his sword on his shoulder, instead of holding it in his hand.—The variation being so trivial, and the point of time and persons just the same, I by no means thought it necessary to engrave more than one of these pictures.

And forthwith taking his filver crofs in his own hands (a thing ftrange and unheard-of before) enters armed therewith into the king's prefence, though earneftly diffuaded by all that wifhed him well. Wherewith the king enraged, commanded his peers to fit in judgment on him, as on a traytor and perjured perfon; and accordingly they adjudged him to be apprehended and caft into prifon. The earls of Cornwall and Leicefter, who fat as judges, citing him forthwith to hear his fentence pronounced, he immediately appealed to the See of Rome, as holding them no judges competent: whereupon all reviling him with the name of traytor and the like, he replied, that, were it not for his function, he would enter the duel or combat with them in the field, to acquit himfelf both of treafon and perjury. This faid, he left the court, and went without delay into Flanders, difguifed, under the name of Dereman."

Over this illumination, in the original, is written this verfe:

Henricus, natus Matildis, Regna tenebat.
Sub quo fanctus Thomas mucrone cadebat.

"Henry, born of Matilda, held the kingdom. In whofe reign faint Thomas was flain with the fword."

The king's robe is blue, lined with light red; his under garment is a deep red: the robe of Becket is a light pink, the darker colour under it is a deep red, and under that is linen: the firft foldier is in blue, and his fword is red; the other is a light red; and their armours are a kind of light lead colour, with a gold back ground.

No IX.

No. IX.

THE MURDER OF THOMAS BECKET.

The arrogance of Becket, however, coſt him his life; for Henry was at laſt ſo highly provoked at his proceeding, that he let fall ſome words, publicly, which ſhewed his diſcontent that he was ſtill living to offend him. Theſe ſpeeches being overheard by four knights, named Sir Hugh Moreville, Sir William Tracy, Sir Richard Britaigne, and Sir Reginald Fitz Urſe, they ſet out with a determination to put an end to his life.—The manner of his death is thus related by Hollingſhed:

"At lengthe the knights, with their ſervauntes, having fought the palace, came ruſhing into the churche by the cloyſter dore, with their ſwordes drawen, ſome of them aſkynge for the traytor, and ſome of them for the archbyſhoppe, who came and mette them, ſaying, Here am I, no traytor, but the archebyſhoppe. The formoſt of the knightes ſayde unto him, Flee! thou art but deade. To whome the archbiſhop ſaide, I will not flee. The knight ſtepte to hym, taking him by the ſleeve, and with his ſworde caſt his cappe beſides hys heade, and ſayde, Come hither, for thou art a priſoner. I will not, ſayde the archebiſhope; doe with me here what thou wilt; and plucked his ſleeve with a mighty ſtrength out of the knight's hand, wherewith the knight ſtepped back two or three paces. Then the archebiſhope, turning to one of the knights, ſayde unto him, What meanethe this, Reygnolde? I have done unto thee many hygh pleaſures, and comeſt thou now unto me into the church armed! Unto whom the knyght anſwer'd and ſayde, Thou ſhalt know anone what is ment: thou art but deade: it is not poſſyble for thee to longer live. Unto whom the archbiſhoppe ſayde, And I am redy to dye for my God, and for the defence of his juſtice and the lybertye of the churche: gladdely do I imbrace death, ſo that the churche may purchaſe peace and lybertye in the ſhedding of my bloode. And herewith takyng on other of the knights by the habergeon, he flung him from him with ſuch violence, that he hadde almoſte throwne him downe to the grounde. Thys was Syr Wylliam Tracye, as he himſelfe did after confeſſe. After this the archbiſhoppe inclyned his heade after the manner of one that ſhoulde pray, pronouncing theſe his laſte wordes: Unto God and to ſaint Marye, and to the ſaintes that are patrons of this churche, and to ſaint Deniſe, I commende my ſelfe and the churches caufe.—Therewyth Sir Reignalde Fytze Urfe ftrykynge a full blowe at his heade, chaunced to light upon the arme of a clerke named Edwarde of Cambridge, who cafte up hys arme to fave the archbyfhoppe; but when he was not able to beare the weight of the blowe, he plucked his arme backe, and fo the ftroke ftayed upon the archbyfhoppe's head, in fuch wyfe that the bloude ran downe hys face: and then they ftroke at hym one after another, and thoughe he fell to the grounde at the feconde blow, they left hym not till they had cutte and tourned out his braines, and ftrowed them about the churche pavement; which done, they went to the ryfling of his houfe, fpoyled all his goods, and tooke them to their own ufes, fuppofing it lawfull for them fo to doe, being the kinges fervauntes."

The original of this plate is a frontifpiece to the Life of Becket. The book is very old, and was moft probably written foon after his death *.

The robe of the archbifhop is blue, with a red crofs and lining; the bottom, being linen, is white. The man with the fword is in a light pink, lined with white; his fleeves are black, and the cap on his head is red: the other man is in green, with red ftockings. The front of the altar-piece is blue, the curtains are green, both ornamented with gold flowers; and the back ground is blue and gold fquares.

* See the Cottonian Catalogue, in which the author is faid to have been either William Fitz Stephen or John Carnotenfem. This MS. contains feveral other Tracts, and is marked Julius A XI.

No. X.

ANTIQUITIES OF ENGLAND.

No. X.
RICHARD THE FIRST.

THE illuminator has here given us two portraits of this valiant prince; and the hiftory relative to them he has written underneath as follows:

Apres Henry le fecund, regna Richard fun fis, x. auns e demy. Il enzepapraud de la tere feynt, fuift pris del duke de Oftris, par ey del Roy Phylippe de Fraunce. E juft reyne hors de prifon pur cent mil liberes de argent; e put cel rauncun, furent les Chalis de Engletere pris des Eglifes e vendus.—Puis fuft tzet de un quazel de Albaft al Chaftel de Chalezun, dunt cefte bers fu fet:

Chrifte, tui Calicis praedo fit praeda Calucis.

" After Henry the Second, reigned Richard his fon, ten years and a half. As he returned from the Holy Land, he was taken by the duke of Auftrich, aided by king Philip of France. He was delivered out of prifon for the [fum of] one hundred thoufand pounds of filver; and for the payment of this ranfom the chaliffes were taken from the churches in England, and fold.—After, he was flain by an arrow from a crofs-bow at the caftle of Chalezun, whence this verfe was made :

" Chrift, thy cup is made the prey of the robbers."

The circumftances of Richard's imprifonment are thus fet down by Holingfhed :

" King Richard having concluded with Saladine, tooke the fea, and comming againe into Cypres, fent his wife, queen Berengaria, with his fifter Joan, late queen of Sicell, into Englande, by the long feas; but himfelf not minding to lye long upon the feas, determined to take his courfe into Grecia, and fo by land paffe homewardes with all fpeed poffible. Howbeit, ere he could attain his purpofe, his chanunce was to be dryven by tempeft upon the coaft of Iftria, not far from Aquilea, where he ftood in fome doubt of his life; for if hee had been knowne and taken, they would furely have kylled him. He therefore made the beft fhift he could to get away, which with fome difficulty he did; and finally, comming to Vien in Oftriche, and there caufing his fervants to provide meate for him, more fumptuous and fine than was thought neceffary for fo mean a perfon as he counterfeyted then to bear the countenaunce of, it was fufpected that he was fome other fort of man than what he fhewed himfelf to be; and in fine,

D 2   thofe

thofe that marked more diligently the manner of him, perceived what he was, and gave knowledge to the duke of Auftrich, named Leopolde, being then in the cityc of Vienna, what they had feene. His page that had the Teutch tongue, goyng aboute the towne to chaunge golde and buye victuals, bewrayed him, having by chaunce the king's gloves under his girdle; whereupon comming to be examined, for fear of tortures, he confeffed the truth. The duke ftreight wayes caufed the houfe where the kynge lodged to be fett about with armed meue, and fente other into the houfe to apprehende him. The kyng, being ware that he was difcried, gotte himfelf to his weapon; but they advifing him to be contented, and alledging the duke's commaundement, hee boldly anfwered, that fithe he muft be taken, he being a king, woulde yeeld himfelfe to none of the companie but to the duke himfelfe, and therefore if it woulde pleafe him to come, he woulde yeelde himfelfe into his handes. The duke hearing of this, fpeedily came unto hym, whom he meeting, delivered his fworde, and committed him unto his cuftodie.—The duke rejoycing of fuch a prey, brought him unto his palace, and with gentle wordes enterteyned him, thoughe hee ment no greate good towards him, as well ynoughe appeared in that he committed to the keeping of certayne gentlemen, which wythout muche curtefie looked ftreightly ynough to him for ftarting awaye, infomuch that they kept hym in colde irons, as fome authors do wryte.—He was taken, as is above defcribed, in December, upon St. Thomas's even, the yeare of our Lord 1192, the fourth of his own reign."

The fecond part of the picture reprefents the death of this monarch, that was occafioned by a wound in the fhoulder which he received whilft he was befieging a town called Chaluz; for in the year of our Lord 1193, the 26th of March, whilft king Richard, together with captain Marchades, went unadvifedly to view the town, the better to confider the place, a crofs-bow man fhot at the king, who hearing a bow fhot off, ftooped down to avoid the blow, and the arrow ftruck him in the fhoulder; and his wound being unfkilfully handled by the furgeon who attended him, he died under his hands foon after. The name of this archer was Bertram de Gurdon, who being afterwards brought to the king, he pardoned him, and alfo ordered one hundred fhillings to be given to him; but when the king was dead, Marchades caufed him to be firft flead alive, and then hanged.

This is from the fame MS. as No. II. and coloured as there defcribed.

No. XI.

IX

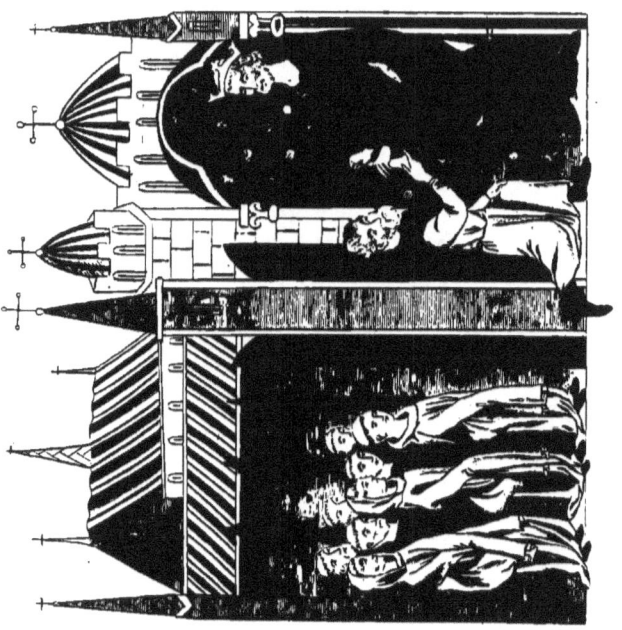

No. XI.

JOHN,

IN his robes of ſtate, receiving a cup (ſuppoſed to contain poiſon) from a monk. Under him is this writing:

Apres Richard, regna Jon ſun frere; en kp ceus Engletere fuiſt entredut vi aunz, e iii quarters, e i mops, par la Pape Innocent, pur meſtre Ciſe en de Laugenton, ke la Rop ne bout receptre a Ereebeke de Kaunterbyrs. Si eſtoyt dunke le graut guere entre lp e les Barons nortaps: duut veeut Sir Lowps, fiz le Rop Phylippe de Fraunce, en Engletere. Le Rop Jon regna xvii aunz e demp, puis veeut a Swyneſheude, e fuſt empoyſone par une frere de la meſon, Il come fu dit, e ſe morut a Newerke, e ſun cors fuſt entere a Wpiceſtre.

"After Richard, reigned John his brother; in whoſe time England was excommunicated [the ſpace of] ſix years, three quarters, and one month, by Pope Innocent, in the cauſe of maſter Stephen Langeton, whom the king would not receive as archbiſhop of Canterbury. Then was the great war between him [the king] and the barons: then alſo came Sir Lewis, the ſon of Philip king of France, into England.—King John reigned ſeventeen years and a half, when coming to Swinſhed, he was poiſoned by a brother of that houſe, as it was reported; and he died at Newark, and his body was buried at Worceſter."

Thus far our French author, who wrote in the reign of Edward the Firſt: and at that time we find the ſtory of the poiſoning of king John was believed indeed, but only confirmed by popular report. However, the ſtory itſelf is ſet down more at large in Grafton (copied from Caxton's book intituled Fructus Temporum, and the Polychronicon) as follows:

"In the ſelf-ſame yere [viz. 1215] king John came to Swineſtede abbey, not farre from Lyncolne; he reſted there two dayes, where he was moſt trayterouſly poyſoned by a monke of the ſame abbey, being of the order of St. Barnard, called Simon Swyneſted. This monke hearyng the king upon an occaſion to talke of breade, and ſay, that if he lived a yere longer he would make that lofe of breade, beyng then of the value of one halfepeny, woorth twelve pence; meayning that he woulde ſo perſecute his rebellious people,

people, that he would not leave one of them to be the owner of a plough. The monke hearyng the king thus fpeake, conceived a bad opinion of him, and goyng forthwith to his abbot, fhewed him the whole matter, and what he was mynded to do. He alleged for himfelfe the prophecie of Cayphas, faiyng, It is better that one man dye, then all the people fhould perifhe. I am well content, fayth he, to die and to become a martyr, fo that I may utterly deftroy this tyrant. With that the abbot wept for gladnefs, and much commended his fervent zeale, as he took it.—The monke beyng then abfolved by his abbot, before-hand, for the doing of this act, went fecretly into the gardeyne upon the backefyde of the abbey, and findynge there a moft venemous toade, he fo pricked him and preffed him with his penne knyfe, that he made him vomit all the poifon that was within him. This done, he conveyed it into a cup of wine, and with a fmyling countenance brought it to the kynge, faying, " If it fhall lyke your princely majeftie, here is a cup of fuch excellent wine as ye never dranke before in all your life-time. The kynge than bid him drink firft, which he chearfully did a large draught; and the kynge alfo drank of the wine.—The monk anone after went to the farmory, and there died, his bowels burfting from his belly; and he had continually from thence three monkes to fing maffes for his foule, confirmed by their general chapter.—The king within fhorte fpace after feeling great griefe in hys body, afked for Simon the monke, and aunfwere was made, that he was departed this lyfe: Then God have mercy upon me! (faid the king) I fufpected as muche.—With that he commaunded his chariot to be brought, for he was not able to ride on horfe-back; fo he went from thence to Slaford caftell, and from thence again to Newarke upon Trent, where in lefs than three days he died, and was ho-nourably buried at Worcefter, with all his armed men attendyng upon his buryall."

This is from the fame MS, and coloured in the fame manner as the former.

No. XII.

No. XII.

HENRY THE THIRD.

THE coronation of Henry the Third. The king is reprefented as holding in his hand a model of Weftminfter Abbey, which he enlarged, laying the firft ftone himfelf; and caufed to be there erected the magnificent monument of Edward the Confeffor. It was very common with the old illuminators, to make the principal figure holding a model of the abbey, or monaftery, they were benefactors to. This prince was crowned the 28th of October, by Peter bifhop of Winchefter, and Joceline bifhop of Bath.

The author gives this hiftory of him:

Apres Jon regna Henry le Teiz, fun fiz, 56 annz; fe fuift de ix aunz de age quant fuft coione. E en fun tens fuft la bataylle de Evefhame, ou fuft occys fyr Symund de Munfort, e fun fiz Henry; e fyre Hugh le Defpenfer, e muz Baronfe des Chevalers de Engleterre.—Puis moruft cyl Henry le Roy, e gift a Weftminfter.

" After John, reigned Henry the Third, his fon, 56 years; and he was but nine years of age when he was crowned. In his time was the battle of Evefham, where was flain Sir Simon de Mountfort, and his fon Henry; and Sir Hugh le Defpenfer, and many barons and knights of England.—After died this Henry the king, and lies [buried] at Weftminfter."

This dreadful battle between the barons and Edward prince of Wales, fon of Henry the Third, is thus more fully defcribed by Holingfhed:

" The laft day of July, A. D. 1265, prince Edwarde with his hoft came to Kenelworth aforefayd, and there fighting with the fayde Simon de Mountforde and his army, with little flaughter difcomfitted the fame, and tooke prifoners the earle of Oxford, the lords William de Mount Chency, Adam de Newmarche, Baldwine Wake, and Hugh Nevill, withe divers other: the lorde Simon himfelfe fledde into the caftell, and fo efcaped. In this mean while, the earle of Leicefter havyng raifed his power, came to the caftell of Munmouth, which the earle of Gloucefter had lately taken and fortified: but they that were within it beeing driven to yielde, it was now rafed down to the ground. This done, the earle of Leicefter entring into Glamorganfhire, and joyning his power withe the prince of Wales, wafted and brent the lands of the fayde earle of Gloucefter: but hearing that his adverfaries

wente

wente about in other places, he returned from thence, and came forwarde towards the ſaide prince Edwarde, who likewiſe made towards him, and at Eveſham they met the ſixth daye of Auguſt, where was foughten a right fierce and cruell battayle betwixte the parties.—As ſome write, the earle of Leiceſter placed kyng Henry in the front of his battel, whome he had there with him as captive, and had arrayed him in his owne coate armour, that if fortune went againſt him, whileſt the enemies ſhould be earneſt to take the K. bearing the ſemblaunce of the chief captayne, he might himſelf eſcape: but king Henry, when they came to joine, fought not, but called to his people, and declared who he was, whereby he eſcaped the daunger of deathe; for being knowen of them, he was ſaved. The Welchmen, which in great numbers the earle of Leiceſter had there on his ſide at the firſte onſett, fled and ranne away, which their demeanor when the earle ſawe, he exhorted thoſe that there were about him to play the men; and ſo ruſhing forth into the preaſe of his enemies, he was encloſed aboute and ſlaine, togither with his ſonne Henry. Hereupon his death being knowen, hys people tooke them to flight, as men utterly diſcomfitted.—There dyed in that battell about 4000 men, as Polidor hathe: but Richard Southwell faith, that there were killed of knightes, or rather men of armes, 180, and of yeomen and dimelances 220, of Welchmen 5000, and of ſuch footmen as were of the earle of Leiceſter's owne retinue, 2000: ſo that there dyed in all to the number of tenne thouſand men, as the ſame Southwell affirmeth. Among which of noblemen theſe are reckoned: Hugh Spencer, lord chief juſtice, the lord Raulf Baſſet, the lord Peter de Mourtford, the lord Beauchampe, Sir Williame Yorke, the lord Thomas de Eſterly, the lord Walter de Creppings, Guy de Bailioll, and the lord Roger Saint John, the lord Robert Tregoz, and other.—This ruine fell to the barons by the diſcord which was ſproong up lately before, betwixt the earles of Leiceſter and Glouceſter, through the inſolency and pride of the earle of Leiceſter's ſonne, who, as I ſayde before, deſpiſing other of the nobility, ſpake many reproachfull wordes by the ſayde earle of Glouceſter, and uſed him in ſuch evill ſorte that he, upon diſpleaſure thereof, hadde not only procured the ſcape of prince Edwarde, but joyned with him in ayde, agaynſte the ſayde earle of Leiceſter and other of the barons, to the utter confuſion both of them and their cauſe."

This plate alſo is from the ſame MS. and coloured as the former.

No. XIII.

EDWARD THE FIRST,

Is here reprefented feated on his throne, and anfwering the pope's bull, which is prefented to him by the archbifhop of Canterbury, and others of the clergy, on the behalf of his holinefs.

What the French author may have faid concerning this prince cannot be difcovered, for the letters at the bottom of this drawing are entirely obliterated; but moft likely he gave fome fhort account of the important and interefting fcene which he has delineated. A full account, however, is here fubjoined, as taken from Speed's Chronicle.

"But in the matter of Scotland, the king, not to feem altogether to neglect the court of Rome, addreffed thither the earle of Lincolne, and the lord Hugh de Spencer, with manifold complaints againft the Scots, and juftification of his owne proceedings: howbeit, at the pope's requeft, hee granted them truce from Hollonmafs to Whitfuntide.

"The juftice of the Englifh armes againfte the Scots, being now againe directly impunged by the papall letters, comprehending fundry arguments on the behalfe of that nation, king Edward, in a parliament at Lincolne, publifhed their contents, and, by confent of the whole reprefentative body of the realme, returned a copious defence of his whole proceedings, with proteftation, firft, that he did not exhibite any thing as in forme of judgement, or tryall of his caufe, but for fatisfaction of his holy father-hood's confcience, and not otherwife. But whereas the pope had required the king to ftand to his decifion for matter of claim, he writes that thereunto he would make an anfwere, as having left that point to the earles and peeres of this land: who, with one minde, directly fignify, that their king was not to anfwere in judgement for any rites of the crowne of England before any tribunall under heaven, and that (by fending deputies or attourneyes to fuch an end) he fhould not make the faid truth doubtfull, becaufe it manifeftly tended to the difinherifon of the faid crowne, whiche they, with the helpe of God, would refolutely, and with all their force, maintain againft all men.—That the refolution of thefe worthy pillars thus in cafe of their countries, crowne, and dignities, may be imitated in their following pofterities, and celebrated in our everlafting remembrances, we (fays mine author) hold it here fit to record their names, fubfcribed in their anfweres unto pope Boniface, dated at Lincolne, in the yeare of our Redemption 1301, and 29 of king Edward the Firfte."

After follows the lift of 100 peers of the realm, who fubfcribed their names to the fupport of the authority of their prince.—Speed then goes on,

"Pope Boniface thus feeing the refolutions of thefe lords, and having enough to doe againfte the French, proceeded no further in thefe bufineffes, but let fall his action, and left the Scots to defend themfelves as they could."

This is the laft illumination in the French MS, fo often quoted, and it is coloured like the former, which is taken from the fame book.

No. XIV.

XIV

No. XIV*.

EDWARD THE SECOND.

THIS plate reprefents king Edward giving a commiffion to Thomas of Brotherton, appointing him marfhal of England.—Over it is written:

Literae R. Edwardi, conftituentes Thomam de Brotherton, Comitem Nottingham, Marefcallum Anglie.

"Letters of king Edward, conftituting Thomas of Brotherton, earl of Nottingham, marfhal of England."

Edward the Second was a very unfortunate prince. His connections were fuch as were not only very improper for a king, but extremely difagreeable to his fubjects in general, and in the end proved his ruin; for having provoked the peers to fuch a degree, they univerfally rofe againft him, and deprived him of his crown firft, and afterwards of his life, and that in a cruel manner. It is true, his death was caufed chiefly by the machinations of Ifabell his wife, Roger Mortimer earl of March, and the bifhop of Hereford.

"The queen (fays Stow) taking it grievoufly that her hufband's life (which fhe deadly hated) was prolonged, made her complaint to her fchoolmafter, ADAM de Orleton, feigning that fhe had certaine dreams, the interpretation whereof fhe mifliked; which, if they were true, fhe feared, left if her hufband be at any time reftored to his old dignity, that hee would burne her for a traytor, or condemne her to perpetuall bondage.—In like fort the bifhop, being guilty in his own confcience, ftood in like feare.—The like feare alfo ftroke the hearts of other for the fame offence: wherefore it feemed good to many of great dignity and bloud, as well fpiritual as temporall, both men and women, that all fuch feare fhould be taken away, defiring his death; whereupon there were letters colourably written to the keepers of Edward, greatly blaming them, for looking fo flenderly to the king, fuffering him to have fuch liberty, and nourifhing him too delicately—

---

* This illumination is in a MS. in the Cotton library, and marked Nero, D. 6.

moreover, there is a privy motion made unto them, but yet in fuch fort, as it might feeme half done, that the death of Edward would not be mifliking to them, wether it were naturell or violent.—And in this point, the greate deceit of fophifters ftood in force, fet downe by the bifhop, who wrote thus:

>Edvardum occidere nolite timere, bonum eft.
>" Kill Edward do not feare, it is a good thing."

Or thus:

>" To feeke to fhed king Edward's blood
>" Refufe,—to feare I count it good."

Which fophiftical faying is to be refolved into two propofitions, whereof the firft, confifting of three words, to wit, Edvardum occidere nolite, " doe not kill king Edward," and the fecond of other three, that is, timere bonum eft, " to feare is a good thing," doe feem fubtilly to difwade from murthering the king; but the recievers of thefe letters, not ignorant of the writing, changed the meaning thereof to this fence, Edvardum occidere nolite timere, " to kill king Edward do not feare," and afterwards thefe words, bonum eft, " it is good:" fo that they, being guilty, turned a good faying into evil.— And fo the keepers, when they had received this letter, put the unfortunate king to a cruel death.

Thomas of Brotherton, who is alfo here reprefented, was the fifth fon of king Edward the Firft, by Margaret his fecond wife. He was born June the firft, A. D. 1300. He was earl of Norfolk (fays Speed) and earl marfhal of England; which earldoms the laft earl, Roger Bigod, having no iffue at his death, left to the difpofition of the king.

This curious painting is drawn from the initial letter of the grant, and is richly emboffed with gold, and elegantly coloured. The king fits on a light red throne, dreffed in a blue robe lined with ermine, his arms and his hofe are red, and his fhoes are a darkifh brown. The armour of Thomas of Brotherton is a light blue, except the body, which is painted red, and the lion argent, and the joints of the armour at the elbows and knees, which are gold. The back ground is a deep fea green; the letter is white, fhaded with red, enclofed in a gold fquare.

No. XV.

No. XV.

EDWARD THE THIRD, AND PRINCE EDWARD.

We have here exhibited the portraits of two of the moſt famous perſonages that our whole annals can boaſt of. To theſe noble heroes we owe the conqueſt of France, the monarch of which kingdom was taken priſoner, at Poictiers, by the prowefs of prince Edward (for his martial deeds ſirnamed the Black Prince) and brought in triumph through the ſtreets of London.—An Engliſhman muſt view this ancient delineation with the greateſt pleaſure, eſpecially when he recollects how much honour and conſequence they gave to their native realm.

King Edward is repreſented giving to his ſon, the Black Prince, the conquered provinces of France.—Over the grant is written,

Donatio principatus Acquitaniae, Franciae, per R. Edwardum, Edwardo Principi Walliae, filio ſuo.

"The donation of the principality of Aquitaine, in France, by king Edward, to Edward prince of Wales, his ſon."

The illuminator has very properly drawn theſe great men in their armour, the bodies of which are adorned with the royal arms of England, quartered with thoſe of France; which bearing was firſt adopted by this noble king.—Of king Edward we have another portrait in the courſe of the work, and the likeneſs of the face in both, may prove their being real portraits. It is alſo neceſſary to give ſome proof that the picture of the Black Prince is equally authentic.

This picture, like the foregoing, No. XIV. is drawn in the initial letter of the original grant, and is finiſhed with great care and labour.—In another MS. (viz. Domitianus, A. XVII. which is alſo in the Cottonian library) is a curious miſſal, formerly belonging to king Richard the Second (who was the ſon of Edward the Black Prince) and was his own maſs-book, uſed by him: it is ſaid to have been wrote for, and preſented to him in his infancy: it is moſt elegantly written, and beautifully illuminated, and contains ſeveral paintings very highly finiſhed, in one of which is a portrait of his father, preſenting him (on his knees) to Our Saviour and the bleſſed Virgin. The

face,

face, the character, and the manner of the hair of prince Edward, are precisely the same as in the illumination I have given, which shews they were either done from the life, or from some picture of him then extant.—I did not engrave the other painting of the Black Prince, because, as the subject seems to be entirely allegorical, I might be therefore thought to break in on my proposed historical series; and it was the less necessary, as the illumination which I have copied is equally as well executed.

The colours of the above illumination are as follows: The king sits on a throne of marble, ornamented with a frame of gold; the armour of both the king and prince is silver, done over with a kind of lacquer, except the joints at the knees and elbows, which are gold; the arms of England are painted on the bodies of their armour in the proper colours; the letter is white, shaded with blue and red, on an entire back ground of gold *.

* The original of this plate is to be found in Nero, D. VI. à MS. in the Cotton Library.

No. XVI.

XVI

ANTIQUITIES OF ENGLAND.

No. XVI.

JOHN OF GAUNT, DUKE OF LANCASTER.

JOHN of Gaunt was the 4th fon of Edward the Third: he was born at Gaunt, a chief town of Flanders, A. D. 1340. In his childhood he was created earl of Richmond, which title was afterwards recalled in, and beſtowed upon John duke of Britanny. He firſt married Blanch, daughter and ſole heir of Henry duke of Lancaſter (fon of Edmund ſirnamed CROUCH BACK) in whoſe right he was firſt earl, and after duke of the fame. By this lady he had iſſued Henry earl of Derby, after duke of Hereford, and laſtly king of England. Beſides the dukedom of Lancaſter, John of Gaunt was earl of Leiceſter, Derby and Lincoln, and high ſteward of England.— This prince is here delineated in the habit of high ſteward of England, examining the right, and granting the commiſſions of the offices claimed by the nobility at the coronation of Richard the Second.

This coronation was extremely grand and magnificent. Speed has copied an account of all the different claims then made, from the very MS. that contains the original of the preſent plate. I have given the following extract from that author, which includes as much of it as is neceſſary to explain the (above-mentioned) illumination:

" John, the king's eldeſt uncle, under the ſtile of John king of Caſtile and Leon, and duke of Lancaſter, by humble petition to the king, claimed to be now ſteward of England, in right of his earldome of Leiceſter ; and, as he was duke of Lancaſter, to beare the king's chiefe ſword, called curtana ; and, as earle of Lincolne, to cut and carve at the royall table before the king. His petitions being found juſt, were confirmed to him, and to his aſſignes, the two earles of Derby and Stafford, the firſt to beare the ſword, while the duke ſhould be buſied about other offices as ſteward, and the other to cut and carve. The duke then, in great eſtate, held this the king's high court of ſtewardſhip, in the Whitehall of the king's pallace at Weſt-minſter, neere to the chappell of the ſaid palace, upon the Thurſday before the coronation, which was alſo upon a Thurſday. There Thomas of Wood-ſtocke, the king's uncle, was admitted to exerciſe the office of conſtable of England,

England, in right of his wife, one of the daughters and heires of Humfrey de Bohun, late earle of Hereford, and conftable of England. Henry de Piercie* was, by the king's confent and writ, authorifed to exercife the place of marfhall of England for that time, faving to every one their right ; for that, by reafon of the time's fhortneffe, the claime which Margaret, daughter and heire to Thomas of Brotherton, late earle of Norfolke, and marfhall of England, laid thereunto, could not be difcuffed."—With various other claims of lefs confequence, made at the fame time ; for which the reader is referred to Speed himfelf.

It is highly probable that the figure kneeling is Thomas of Woodftock, high conftable of England. This Thomas was the feventh and youngeft fon of Edward the Third, and brother to John of Gaunt.

He is dreffed in dark blue and white ; the figure kneeling is in dark blue and red; the feat a kind of pink, and the back ground red ; the letter half blue, and half red, worked on with white, and blue corners, with a gold edge round the whole †.

* Or de Percy (fo the name was originally written). PERCY is a town in Lower Normandy, where this great family had their place of refidence before the Conqueft.
† This is in Nero, D. vi.

XVII

THE two fucceeding plates are taken from illuminations in a large MS. at Weftminfter Abbey. The following is a concife account of the book itfelf:

" The book commonly called Liber Regalis, is a large and curious miffal, which, by the arms emblazoned in it, feems to have been procured, and prefented to the church of Weftminfter, by Nicholas Lytlington, who was abbot there from 1362 to 1386.

" Befides the ufual calendar, rubric, and offices of thofe times, it contains an exact ordinal of the fervice and ceremonies then ufed at the coronation of the kings and queens-confort; together with the chants and anthems performed on the occafion. And the illumination prefixed to this ceremonial, bearing a near refemblance to the portrait of Richard the Second, in the choir of Weftminfter, renders it highly probable that this curious book was provided for the direction of the prelates and nobles who affifted at that prince's coronation, July the 16th, 1377, and thence acquired the name of Liber Regalis.

" Note, In the catalogue of the Harleian MSS. No. 310-xiv. fome particulars, touching the coronation of the kings and queens, are faid to have been collected out of a book called Liber Regalis, in the treafury of the church of Weftminfter; probably by Sir Simon D'Ewes, who made a large collection of MSS. relating to Englifh hiftory.

" It is likewife fuppofed that a copy of the above-mentioned ceremonial was taken from it while lord keeper Williams was dean of Weftminfter, which may ftill be in private hands."

No. XVII.

THE CORONATION OF RICHARD THE SECOND.

THIS prince, at the death of his grandfather, king Edward (which happened in the month of June, 1377) was but eleven years of age, and on the 16th of July, in the fame year, was folemnly crowned king of England by Simon Sudbury, archbifhop of Canterbury, affifted by abbot Lytlington. The earl of Derby (afterwards king Henry IV.) bears the curtana.—See page 31.

REGAL AND ECCLESIASTICAL

"At this coronation (fays Speed) Thomas of Woodſtocke, youngeſt ſon of deceaſed king Edward, was created earle of Buckingham, Thomas Mowbray earle of Nottingham, Guychard d'Angolem earl of Huntingdon, and Henry de Piercy earl of Northumberland.—Thus (adds he) the bountie of the young monarch imparted large rays of his imperiall ſplendour to theſe eminent perſons of his kingdome: howeſoever, theſe and like honours have not in our common wealth eyther alwayes beene fortunate to the receivers, or without repentance to the donors."

The king's robe is gold, his cloſe garment pink and gold flowers; the throne is a reddiſh brown; the biſhop at the right hand is in white, and a blue robe with gold flowers; the abbot at the left is alſo in white, a gold robe with white ſpots: the earl of Derby is habited in blue, with white hoſe and dark ſhoes; the attendant behind is in white; the croſs, croſier, mitres and other ornaments, as well as the back ground, are gold; the lighter colour of the frame red, the dark part blue.

No. XVIII.

No. XVIII.

THE CORONATION OF HIS QUEEN, ANNE OF BOHEMIA.

TAKE the following account of the fame from Holingſhed:

" News came (ſays that author) that the lady Anne, ſiſter to the emperoure Wenſlaus, and fyanced wife to the kyng of England, was come to Caleis; wherupon the parliamente was prorogued till after Chriſtmaſs, that in the mean time marriage myghte be ſolemniſed, whyche was appointed after the Epiphanye: and forthwith great preparation was made to receyve the bryde, that ſhe myght be conveyed with all honour unto kyng's preſence.

" Suche as ſhoulde receyve hir at Dover, repayred thither, where, at hir landing, a marvellous and righte ſtraunge wonder happened; for ſhee was no ſooner out of hir ſhippe, and got to lande in ſafety with all hir companye, but that forthwith the water was ſo troubled and ſhaken, as the like thing had not in any man's remembrance ever bin hearde of: ſo that the ſhippe in which the appoynted queene came over, was terribly rent into pieces, and the reſidue ſo beaten one agaynſte another, that they were ſcattered heere and there, after a wonderfull manner. Before hir comyng to the citye of London, ſhee was met on Blackheath, by the mair and citizens of London, in moſt honourable wife, and ſo with greate triumph convey'd to Weſtminſter, where at the time appoynted, all the nobilitie of the realme being aſſembled, ſhee was joyned in marriage to the king, and crowned queene, by the archebyſhop of Caunterbury, with all the glory and honour that might be deviſed.

" There were alſo holden, for the more honour of the fame marriage, ſolemne juſtes for certayne dayes together, in which, as well the Engliſhmen as the new queene's countrymen, ſhewed proofe of their manhoode and valiancie, wherby prayſe and commendation of knightly prowes was atchieved, not withoute domage of both the parties."

REGAL AND ECCLESIASTICAL

The queen's garment is blue; the robe gold, lined with ermine; the throne filver varnifhed: both the bifhops are in white, edged with gold; their robes are pink with red flowers, edged with gold; mitres, croffes and the borders are gold: the attendants are white; back ground blue, and the frame gold.

This plate is from the fame MS. with the foregoing.

XIX

No. XIX*.

KING RICHARD THE SECOND.

THIS prince is here reprefented as feated on his throne, furrounded by the different officers of the court, and receiving a book from a monk, intituled

Un pouje et fimple epiftje d'un vieil folitaire des Celeftins de Paris, adreffant a tjes excellent, et tjes puiffant, tjes debonnaire, catholique, et tjes devoft prince Richard, par la grace de Dieu, Roy d'Angleterre, &c.—pour aucune confirmation tele que de la vraye paix et amour fraternelle du dit Roy d'Angleterre, et du Charles, par la grace de Dieu, Roy de France.

In Englifh thus:

" A poor and fimple epiftle of an old folitary of the Celeftins of Paris, addreffed to the moft excellent, and moft powerful, moft polifhed, catholic, and moft devout prince Richard, by the grace of God, king of England, &c.—for no other purpofe than the confirmation of the true peace and fraternal love of the faid king of England and of Charles, by the grace of God, king of France."

I could not get any further intelligence concerning the author of this MS. but it is fairly written, and the picture is well finifhed.

This illumination is very curious, on account of the extraordinary length of the fhoes, then worn at court. That they might not be troublefome to the wearer when he walked abroad, they were faftened up by means of a fmall chain to the knee.

This truly ridiculous fafhion continued a long time in vogue. In the reign of Edward the Fourth (fays Stow) it prevailed univerfally, fo that thofe whofe finances would not allow them chains of gold and filver, had filken ftrings ftretch'd from the knee to the long point of the fhoe. This enormity was at laft taken into the confideration of the parliament, and in the third year of Edward the Fourth it was enacted, that no men fhould

---

* This illumination is in a MS. in the Royal library at the Britifh Mufeum, and mark'd 20. B. 6.

wear shoes, or boots, with pikes exceeding two inches in length. But this regulation was not quite effectual, for in the fifth year of the same prince we find it was proclaimed throughout the kingdom, that no man, of any degree whatsoever, should wear any shoes or boots whose points exceeded two inches, upon pain of cursing by the clergy, besides the forfeiture of twenty shillings. After this last act, we hear no more of them.

The king's robe is blue, lined with ermine; the throne is of a light stone colour, with the arms of England proper. The monk is dressed in a dark pink; his book is gold, the flag white with a red cross, and the lamb gold. The figure behind the monk is dressed in a light blue. The nobleman at the right hand of the picture is in red and gold, the dark leg blue, the other white. The next figure has on a light pink robe, lined with white; his legs are red. The monk behind the throne is in blue, and the other figure is in a light flesh-coloured robe: the pavement a light red, and the back ground blue and gold.

ANTIQUITIES OF ENGLAND. 39

THIRTEEN of the following illuminations are taken from a curious MS. on vellum*, containing the history of the latter part of the reign of (that unfortunate monarch) king Richard the Second, beginning April the 25th, 1399, and ending upon the delivering up of Isabel, the young queen of England, widow of Richard the Second, to the commissioners of her father, Charles the Sixth, king of France.

This book was written by Francis de la Marque, a French gentleman who was in the suit of the king during his troubles, and was formerly in the library of the count de Maine.

As the following explanations of these pictures are but short, I refer the curious reader to Stow, in whose Chronicle he will find this latter part of the life and reign of Richard (beginning with his going to Ireland) word for word taken from this author: it appears also that Holingshed made use of him; but neither of them make the least mention of him.

The reverend Dr. Percy, in a MS. note which he has prefixed to the original book, speaks of the illuminations in the following manner:

" The several illuminations contained in this book are extremely curious and valuable, not only for the exact display of the dresses, &c. of the time, but for the finished portraits of so many eminent characters as are preserved in them."

No. XX.

THE author paying his respects to a Gascoigne knight (undoubtedly the same whom Holingshed and Stow name Janico D'Artois) who, he tells us, requested him to go with him to England: he accordingly went with him from Paris to London, and thence set out for Ireland to attend king Richard the Second, who was newly gone over to subdue Mac Murrough, the great Irish rebel.

The author himself relates the matter as follows:

> Cinq jours devant le premier jour de May,
> Que chascun doit laisser dueil et esmay,
> Un chevalier que de bon cuer a may,
> Moult doulcement,

---

* This MS. is in the Harleian library at the British Museum, and marked 1319.

> Me dit, amp, Je bous pri cherement,
> Qu'en Albion bueilliez joyeufement
> Abecques moy benir prochainnement,
> Il bueil aler?
> Je refpondi; monfeigneur, commander
> Povez fur moy;—Je fui preft d'encliner
> Ma boulente a botre bon penfer,
> Nen doubtez ja.
> Le chevalier cent foiz me mercia,
> Difant, frere certes il convendra
> Bein brief partir,—car hafter nos fauldra
> Soiez certains.
> Ce fu en lan mil, quatre cens, un mains
> Que de Paris,—chafcun de joie plains,
> Nous partifmes, chevauchant foirs et mains
> Sans otargier
> Jufqua Londres, la nous conbint logier
> Un Mercredi, a heur de mangier;
> La povoit on veoir maint chevalier
> Faire depart
> De la Ville, car le bon Roy Richart
> Eftoit partiz, &c.

Which may be thus tranflated:

" Five days before the firſt day of May, when every one ought to leave off mourning and grief, a knight, with great love towards me, ſaid ſoftly thus, " Friend, I earneſtly beſeech thee, if it pleaſe thee, to go joyfully with me directly to Britain." —I anſwered, " My lord, you may command me; I am ready, doubt not, to incline my will to your deſires."—The knight thanked me a hundred times, and ſaid, " Brother, it will be neceſſary for us to ſet off directly, for be certain we muſt be haſty."—It was in the year one thouſand four hundred, that one morning we ſet out joyfully from Paris, riding day and night, without delay, till we came to London, where we arrived on a Wedneſday at the hour of dinner; and there we ſaw many knights departing from thence, for the good king Richard was already ſet out."

The ſhowy luxurious habit of the knight deſerves attention. When the knights were not caſed in armour, they wore a dreſs that ſeems to have more than Aſiatic ſoftneſs and effeminacy.—He is habited in red and gold; the dark part of the ſleeve is blue, the light part white. The author is in green; the ground proper, and the back ground blue and gold in diamonds.

No. XXI.

XX

ANTIQUITIES OF ENGLAND.

No. XXI.

THE KNIGHTING OF HENRY, SON TO THE DUKE OF LANCASTER.

KING Richard being with his forces in Ireland, confers, with great marks of kindnefs, the order of knighthood on the fon of Henry duke of Lancafter and earl of Derby, then in banifhment. This fon was afterwards king Henry the Fifth.

The author fays as follows:

En ce faifant, le roy, qui les liepars
Porte en blafon, fist rens de toutes pars,
Faire & tancoff pavons & eftandars
En haule lever.
Apres fift, il de vrap cuer, fans amer,
Le fils au duc de Lanceaftre mander,
Qui eftoit bel & jeune bacheler,
Et avenant,
Et puis le fift chevalier, en difant,
Mon beau coufin, foies preu et baillant;
Defore mais car pou abes baillant
Sans conquerir.
Et pour le plus honnorer et cherir,
En actroiffant fon bien & fon plaifir
Affin telle, qu'il en euft fouvenir,
Plus longuement,
En fift d'autres viii. ou dix, &c.

" Whilft this was doing, the king, [Richard] who bears in blazon the leopards *, caufed pavons and ftandards to be fet on high, in every part of the field; after which, with kind heart, without bitternefs, he commanded the fon of the duke of Lancafter, who was a fair young bachelor, to be brought before him, and there made him a knight, faying, " My fair coufin, be brave and valiant; for few are valiant without conquering." And that he might confer the greater honour upon

* Alluding to the arms of England, which were formerly three leopards.

him,

him, and fix this pleafure more laftingly in his mind, he [the king] alfo made eight or ten more knights at the fame time.

The king's garment, and the trappings of his horfe, are red and gold flowers; all the armour and helmets (in this, and through the whole of thefe thirteen illuminations) are of a lead colour. Prince Henry's garment is blue, and the figure behind the king is in blue, and the next to him is red; the trees and the ground proper; the back ground red, with gold ftripes and flowers; the ftandard (which is the arms of England) proper, and the ftreamer blue and gold flowers.

From the fame MS. as the former.

No. XXII.

ANTIQUITIES OF ENGLAND. 43

No. XXII.

INTERVIEW WITH MAC MURROUGH.

Mac Murrough (or, as the French author calls him, Maquemore) is drawn coming forth from between two woods, to meet Thomas Spencer, earl of Gloucester, the king's commander in chief; upon which a conference ensues. The Irish are described as riding without saddle, stirrups, boots, &c.

The author gives the following curious description of the appearance of Maquemore:

Entre deux bois, asses loing de lamer,
Paquemore, la montaigne avaler,
Up & Dirlois; que pas ne scay nombrer
Pot foison.
Un cheval, or sans sele ne arcon,
Qui lui avoit cousté, ce disoiton,
Quatre cens vaches, tant estoit bel et bon;
Car pou d'argent
A on pais, pource comunment
Marchandent eulx a bestes, seulement.
En descendant, couroit si aspremeut
Qua mon advis,
Oncques mais jour de ma ve ne vis
Couree sitost liebre, cerf ne brevis,
D'autre beste, pour certain la vous dis
Comme il faisoit.
En sa main dextre un darde portoit
Grant & longue, de quoy moult bein gettoit.
Sa semblaunce ainsi comme il estoit
Uerz pourtraire.

[Then comes the picture.]

Devant le bois ———
——— la fuit l'assemblee fait
Pres d'un ruissel,

G 2 " Between

REGAL AND ECCLESIASTICAL

"Between two woods, at a diſtance from the ſea, Maquemore, taking the advantage of the mountains, was with his Iriſh; the number I cannot juſtly ſay. He had a horſe (on which he ſat) without ſtirrups or ſaddle, which coſt him, as it was ſaid, four hundred cows, it was ſo valuable; for in that country they have but little money, and merchandize only with beaſts, which they exchange. In deſcending [from the wood towards the king's hoſt] he rode ſo ſwiftly, that in all my life I never ſaw either hare, ſtag, or any other beaſt, able to keep pace with him. In his right hand he carried a great long dart, which he could uſe very dexterouſly. His appearance was as you may here ſee painted.—[Here comes in the picture.]—Before the wood, the aſſembly was made near to a little rivulet."

Mac Murrough has a light pink robe over his ſhoulder; and the figure next to him is in white, with a red cap; and the third figure is red, with a white cap. The middlemoſt figure of the ſoldiers is in red, and the other two in blue; the ground and trees proper, and the back ground blue and gold.

From the ſame MS. as No. XX.

No. XXIII.

THE ARCHBISHOP OF CANTERBURY PREACHING TO THE PEOPLE.

WHILE king Richard is in Ireland, he receives intelligence that Thomas Arundel, archbifhop of Canterbury, had publicly preached of the great wrongs done to Henry duke of Lancafter, and had produced a bull from Rome, promifing Paradife to all that would aid him againft his enemies.

The author fpeaks as follows:

    Et comment quant il arriva primer
    En fon pais, il fift auf gens prechier
    L'arcevefque de Cantorbie fier
    Difant, ainfi,
    Hes bonnes gens, entendes tous ici;
    Tious favez bien comment le Roy Henry
    A grant tort voire feigneur Henry,
    Et fans raifon,
    Et pource fup fait imperzation.
    Au faint Pere, qui eft noftre patron,
    Que treftous ceulx anvont remiffion
    De leur pechies,
    De quop oncques ils furent entachiez,
    De puis l'eure qu'ilz furent baptifiez,
    Qui lui aideront tous certains enfoiez;
    Celle jornee,
    Et vefenci la bulle feelle,
    Que la Pappe de Rome la lovee
    On envoie; & pour vous vous donne,
    Hes bons amis, &c.

Which may be thus tranflated:

" And now, when he [duke Henry] firft arrived in his country, he caufed the archbifhop of Canterbury to preach to the people, faying, " My good friends, all

REGAL AND ECCLESIASTICAL

of you who are here have heard of the evils which the king Richard * hath done to your lord Henry, and that without any reafon. For this caufe I have prayed to faint Peter, who is our patron, that all thofe who fhall aid the duke fhall have fpeedy pardon and remiffion of all their fins, which they may have committed from the hour of their baptifm to the prefent time. And here behold the fealed bull which the Pope of Rome hath fent to me, my good friends, to confirm the fame to you."

The archbifhop's robe is red and gold, his mitre white and gold; the figure holding the crofs is in a lead colour : the firft of the five fitting front figures is in a light pink; the next blue, and his legs white; the next in purple, the next in red, and the laft in green : the other figures are red and blue, the pulpit a light green, the cloth blue and gold, the feal to the bull red, the back ground blue and gold.

This is from the fame MS. with No. XX.

* So it fhould certainly be, though the French author has miftakenly, in the fecond verfe, wrote it " le Roy Henry," inftead of " le Roy Richart," to whom it undoubtedly alludes.

No. XXIV.

No. XXIV.

KING RICHARD WITH HIS FRIENDS AT CONWAY.

King Richard having landed at Milford Haven, is here drawn as consulting with his friends at Conway castle. He seems to wear a priest's black cowl, probably by way of disguise. The person (in blue) speaking to the king, is John Montacute, earl of Salisbury; the bishop (above him) in a cowl, seems to be Merks, bishop of Carlisle. In a separate compartment to the right, are John Holland, duke of Exeter, the king's half-brother, and Thomas Holland, duke of Surrey, son to the king's other half-brother, Thomas Holland, earl of Kent, deceased.—The French author thus describes the scene which he has here depicted:

> A l'assembler du Roy contour,
> En lieu de joie, p'ot moult grant douleur,
> Plenus plains supirs n'y rent pas sejour,
> Gemirs ne duril;
> Certes cestoit grant pitie avoir duril
> Leur countenance & leur mortel acueil,
> La route avoit la face de son mueil
> Desconlourre,
> Au Roy conta sa dure destinee,
> Et comment fait avoit son assemblee,
> Quant descendu fu de la mer sallee
> En Engleterre.

Something like this in English:

"The assembly round about the king, instead of being joyous, were full of grief, so that there was nothing but the mournful appearance of tears, complainings, sighs, and groans; it was a very piteous sight to see the anxiety and grief which was upon their countenances. The earl [of Salisbury] appeared at best but disconsolate, and to the king recounted his cruel destiny, and how he had gathered his host, when he landed from the salt sea into England, &c."

REGAL AND ECCLESIASTICAL

The king is habited in a red robe and black cowl; Salifbury is in blue and gold; the bifhop behind the king is in a fky blue cowl and dark pink robe; the figure at the king's right hand is in light pink and gold, and the other above him in red, with a blue cap. The figures in the other compartment are, the one in a dark blue and gold, and the other in a light red. The buildings of a ftone colour, except the roofs, which are red; the back ground blue and gold.

From the fame MS. as No. XX.

xxv

ANTIQUITIES OF ENGLAND. 49

No. XXV.

THE EMBASSY OF KING RICHARD SENT TO THE DUKE OF LANCASTER.

THE king fends the duke of Exeter and the duke of Surrey to the duke of Lancafter at Chefter, to confer with him, and come to an agreement to terminate their difference. He keeps only fixteen perfons with him at Conway.

The author writes thus:

> Pour envoiez devers le duc Henri,
> Or avvint il que par eulz fu choifi
> Le duc Dercestre, car on enft un faille
> La arjoubez;
> Homme qui sceuft fi fagement parler,
> Ne ungrant fait pronouncier & conter.
> Avecques lui fist le bon Rop alez
> Son beau coufin,
> Qui effoit duc de Soubjap. Le matin
> Partirent, eulz du Rop le quel de fin
> Cuer leur pria de abreger la chemin
> Et de bein faire,
> Et que tresbein lui comptent tout l'affaire
> Que cp devant avez op retraire;
> Affin telle que de lui puiffent traire
> Accoft ou paix.

Thus in Englifh:

" The duke of Exeter was chofen [by the king] to be fent to the duke Henry; for amongft all his company there was none that could fpeak more fenfible, or fet an important affair in a jufter light. With him the king alfo fent his coufin, the duke of Surrey. They fet forth in the morning, and the king earneftly befought them to be fpeedy in their journey, and execute their commiffion with all the care and difpatch that they could; for he fhould be very anxious to know whether peace or war was intended towards him."

H The

REGAL AND ECCLESIASTICAL

The chief figure is in blue and gold, with a red cap and black boots, and the trappings of his horfe are red; the other is in red and gold, and a blue cap, and black trappings; the horfes are of an amber-coloured brown. The principal figure of the attendants is in green (this is the author) and the two on either fide of him in blue, with brown caps; and the light figure is in white, and a red cap. Ground proper, and back ground blue and gold.

From the fame MS. as No. XX.

No. XXVI.

ANTIQUITIES OF ENGLAND.   51

No. XXVI.

THE INTERVIEW WITH DUKE HENRY.

THE dukes of Exeter and of Surrey are introduced to the duke of Lancafter, who is in black, being in mourning (I fuppofe) for the death of John of Gaunt, his father. Henry duke of Lancafter only detains the duke of Exeter, who had married his fifter, but imprifons the duke of Surrey.

The original runs thus:

 Au duc Henry firent ments le pas
 Droit ou chaftel, qui fu fait acompas,
 Au ceur en ot grant joie & grant foulas
 Quant il les vit;
 Tres bonne chiere par femblance leur fift;
 Et puis apres au duc Derceftre dit,
 Or ca beau frere fans plus de contre dit
 De vos nouvelles,
 Je vous fupple, que vous me diez qu'elles,
 Ils font beau frere.—Une font pas tres belles,
 Pour monfeigneur, ains font laides & felles,
 Dont moult doulant.
 Sui et marry et los lui ba comptant
 Treffagement tout ce qu'ey devant,
 Abez op quant ils furent partant
 D'avec le Roy, &c.———

 Le duc Henry les fift en deur partie,
 Avec lui fift fon beau frere tenir,
 La duc Derceftre;
 Et le bon duc de Souldzap fift il mettre,
 Et enfermer ens ou chaftel de Ceftre,
 Qu'il p'a maint belle feneftre,
 Et maint hault mur.

In Englifh:

"And they directed their fteps to the caftle where duke Henry was, who rejoiced extremely when he faw them, and caufed them to be feafted with great pretended amity.

amity. This done, he said to the duke of Exeter, " I beseech thee, fair brother, without the least restraint, to tell me what news you bring."—[He answered] " It is what will not be very pleasing to my lord, but, on the contrary, very distasteful and unhappy."—Then he entered upon his discourse in a most prudent manner, relating the reasons for which he left the king," &c.

[And this he did in so plain and open a manner, and was seconded by Surrey so, that Henry was very angry, and proceeded to violence.]

" The duke Henry ordered them to be parted, and his half-brother, the duke of Exeter, he caused to be kept with him; but the good duke of Surrey was shut up closely in the castle of Chester," &c.

Lancaster is in black; the two dukes as before; the soldier by Lancaster is in a light pink, with gold flowers; the buildings as before, except the roofs, which are blue; the back ground red, striped with gold.

From the same MS. with No. XX.

No. XXVII.

No. XXVII.

INTERVIEW BETWEEN THE EARL OF NORTHUMBERLAND AND KING RICHARD.

THE earl of Northumberland (Henry Percy, firſt earl) comes from duke Henry to perſuade the king to go with him, and delivers his meſſage on his knees. The perſon by the king is the earl of Saliſbury. Northumberland plainly tells the king of the errors of his government, and promiſes him that the differences between him and the duke of Lancaſter ſhall be determined by parliament: this he offers to confirm by oath.

The author ſays:

  Lors le conte monta
  En un vaiſſel & leaue oultre paſſa,
  Le roy Richart ens caſtel trouva,
  Et avec lui
  Trouva le conte de Salſebery,
  Et leſueſque de Ke lille ainſi,
  La diſt au roy—Sire, le duc Henry
  Sarp tamis,
  Atin qu'acoit entre vous deus foit mis,
  Et que foies deſormais bons amis,
  Sil vous plaiſt, ſire, & que ie ſoie oys,
  Je vous diray
  Ce qu'il vous mande ne viens nen mentiray.
  Se vous voules eſtre bon juge & bray,
  Et treſtous ceuls, qui ey vous nommeray,
  Faire venir
  A certain jour, pour juſtice acomplir,
  A Weſtmouſtre, le parlement ovir,
  Que vous feres entre vous deus tenir,
  Par loyaulte;
  Et que grant juge ſoit il reſtitue
  D'engletere, comme l'avoit eſte
  Le duc ſon pere, & tout ſon parente,
  Plus de cent ans,

In Englifh thus:

" The earl [of Northumberland] paffed over the water in a little veffel, and found king Richard in the caftle, and with him the earl of Salifbury, and the bifhop of Carlifle alfo. And he faid to the king, " Sire, the duke Henry hath fent me, that I fhould ufe my endeavour to make an accord between you and him, that henceforth you may be good friends, if it pleafe you to hear me fpeak what I am commanded without deceit.—If you will be a good and true judge, and fpeedily caufe thofe to come fome certain day to Weftminfter, whom I fhall name to you, that juftice may be done between you two there, loyally, in the open parliament; and that the office of great judge [fenefchall, or high fteward] of England fhall be reftored to duke Henry, which was held by the duke his father, and his anceftors, more than one hundred years," &c.

Northumberland is in blue and gold; the king and Salifbury as before; the fmall figure in front is in a light pink, the next in blue, the next blue and gold, and the laft green; the flat roofs red, and the turret tops blue; the back ground blue, flowered with gold.

From the fame MS. with No. XX.

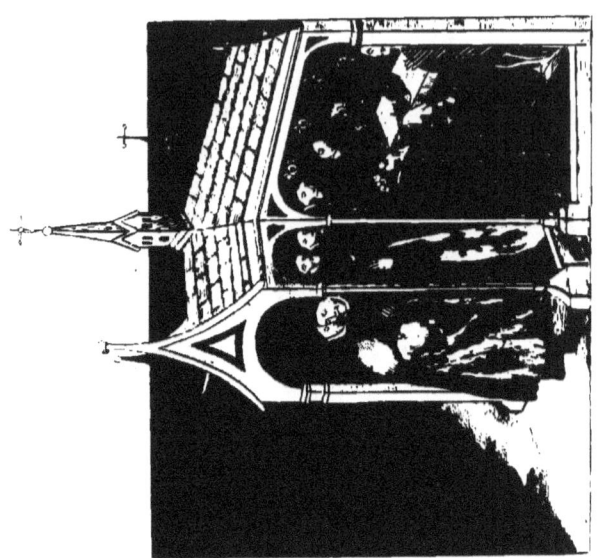

No. XXVIII.

THE ACCORD BETWEEN THE EARL OF NORTHUMBERLAND AND KING RICHARD.

THE earl of Northumberland confirms by solemn oath, and by receiving the sacrament, the truth of his preceding engagement, that the differences between the king and the duke of Lancaster shall be determined in parliament: on which the king consents to go with him.

The author writes as follows:

    Lors respondi le conte, Mon seigneur,
    Faites sacres le corps nostre seigneur,
    Je jurray qu'il n'a point de faveur,
    Once fait ey,
    Et que le Duc le tenra tout tussi
    Que la maves ay comter icy.
    Chascun deuls la devotement oy
    Le messe dire.
    Le counte alors sans, plus riens contredire,
    Fist le serement, sur le corps nostre Sire,
    Elas! le sanc lui devoit bein desrire,
    Car le contraire
    Savoir il bein non obstant voit il faire
    Leserement, tel que moes retraire
    Pour acomplir son valour, & par faire
    Ce que promis
    Avoit au duc, qu'il ot au roy tramis;
    Ainsi firent entreulx leur compromis,
    L'un pensoit mal, & l'autre encores pis.

Which may be thus translated:

"Then answered the earl [of Northumberland] "My lord, make holy the body of our Lord, and I will swear that I have spoke the truth in this matter, and that the duke [of Lancaster] will perform all which I have declared."—Then both the king and the earl heard the mass devoutly. The earl directly after, without the least hesitation, made oath upon the body of our Lord.—Alas! his blood might

56   REGAL AND ECCLESIASTICAL

well run cold, when he knew that the oath was contrary to his intentions, and only taken the better to carry on his defign, in order to perform the promife he had made to betray the king into the hands of the duke ; for promifes had paffed between them, one of them thinking evilly, and the other ſtill worſe."

The figure behind the king is in blue and gold; the perſon with his hand lifted up is in red and gold, a blue ſleeve, and light linen ; the figure without is in pink, and blue legs and feet, and the other difcourfing with him is in blue and gold; the prieſt is in blue ſtriped with gold; the ſtep green, the cup gold, and the altar blue and gold ; the ground proper, and the roof blue ; back ground blue and gold. The king himſelf and Northumberland are habited as before.

No. XXIX.

No. XXIX.

THE KING BETRAYED.

As the king goes towards Chester, he finds a party of soldiers belonging to the earl of Northumberland placed in a valley, the earl (who had gone before) being at their head; who tells the king he had placed these men to guard him to Chester, as the country was all in arms, &c. The king, alarmed, offers to turn back; but the earl dissuades him from a measure which would reflect dishonour upon him, and prevails on him to take some refreshment of bread and wine.

> Jusqua la bille que la roche abaler,
> A la quell batoit la haulte mer,
> D'autre coste on ne poboit passer,
> Pour la rochaille;
> Ainsi comunt passer baille que baille,
> Ou estze moit tout paimp la bataille
> Des gens du conte, qui fu aime de maille
> Et bene buell.

> ―――― Ainsi parlant nous comunt, approchier
> Deuls si comme au trait d'un bon archier,
> Lors le conte se bin, agenoillier
> Tiestoit a terre,
> Disant au rop—Je bous aloie querre,
> Mon droit seigneir, ne bous bueille displere
> Car le pays est es meu pour le guerre
> Com bous sabes,
> Affin que meulx soies assenres,
> Lors dist le roy, il fausse bein alles
> Sans tant de gens qui ey mandes abes.

" They rode from the town till they came to the rock, which on one side was beat by the high sea, and on the other there was no passage because of the rock itself; so that when we had passed from valley to valley, we saw the people of the earl ranged in battle array, armed in coats of mail, ―――

I

Thus

———— Thus speaking amongst ourselves (says the author) we approached to them at the distance of about a bow shot, when the earl came, and fell upon his knees on the ground, saying to the king, " My true lord, be not displeased, for the country is up in arms, as you well know, and these men are for your better guard." —When the king said [for he saw that he was betrayed] " I could well have went without so many people to attend upon me as you have here commanded."

The bishop behind the king in a sky-blue cowl; the figure at the king's right hand pink and gold, and a red cap; the first right-hand soldier blue and gold, the next red, and him behind in pink; the first soldier on the left a dark lead colour, the next pink, the next blue, and the last red; the rock and the ground dark green, back ground blue and red. The king himself as before; as is Northumberland, all except his armour, which is of an iron colour, as are all the armours.

From the same MS. as No. XX.

No. XXX.

INTERVIEW BETWEEN THE DUKE OF LANCASTER AND KING RICHARD.

The king being come to Flint castle, is respectfully saluted by the duke of Lancaster, and there ensues a short conference. To relate this the more exactly, the author (who was present) has put it into prose. As this historical passage is extremely curious, I have given it in the author's own words, as follow:

Apres entra la duc on chastel, arme de toutes pieces excepte de bacinet, comme vous poves veoir en ceste historie; lors sist on descendre le roy, qui avoit desne en donson, & venir a l'encontre du duc Henry, le quel de si loing qu'il l'avisa s'enclina asses bas a terre, et en approuchant l'un de l'autre il s'enclina le second fois, son chapel en sa main. Et lors le roy osta son chapperon, & parla primer, disant en telle maniere:

"Beau cousin de Lancastre, vous soies le tresbien venu."

Lors respondi le duc Henry, encline asses bas a terre,

"Mon seigneur, je sui venu plustoist que vous ne mandes mande; la raison pourquoy je le vous diray.—La commune renommee de votre peuple si est telle, Que vous les aves, par l'espace de 20 ou 22 ans, trete maubaisement et tresrigoreusement goubrines, et tant qu'ils, n'en sont pas une content.—Mais sil plaist a notre seigneur, je le vous aideray a goubernier meulx qu'il na este goubernie le temps passe."

Le roy Richart lui respondi alors,

"Beau cousin de Lancastre, puis qu'il vous plaist il nous plaist bien."

Et sachies de certain, que ce sont le propres paroles qu'ils dirent eulx deux ensemble, &c.

Literally thus in English:

"After the duke entered the castle, armed at all points except the bacinet [helmet] as you may see in this story. Then they caused the king to come down, who had dined in the Keep, that he might meet the duke Henry, who, as far as he saw the king, bowed very low to the ground, and as he approached, he bowed the second time, with his cap in his hand. Then the king put off his hood, and fpake firft, faying in this manner:

"Fair coufin of Lancafter, you are very welcome."

Then anfwered the duke Henry, bowing very low to the ground,

"My lord, I am come fooner than you commanded me; the reafon why I will tell you.—The common fame of your people is this, That you have, for the fpace of 20 or 22 years, treated them fo evilly, and fo very rigouroufly governed them, that there is not one of them contented.—But if it pleafe my lord, I will aid you to govern them better than they have been governed in time paft."

Then the king Richard anfwered,

"Fair coufin of Lancafter, fince it pleafes you, it pleafes us well."

And know for certain, that thefe are the very words which were faid by thofe two together."

The earl of Salifbury is at the king's right hand; Merks, bifhop of Carlifle, at his left.

The bifhop is in a fky blue robe, and pink cowl; the figure next him, at his left, blue and gold; firft foldier behind Lancafter pink, next red; the roofs of the houfes blue, and the turret red; the back ground is red, with gold flourifhes. The king, Lancafter and Salifbury, as before.

This is from the fame MS. as No. XX.

No. XXXI.

No. XXXI.

KING RICHARD CONVEYED TO LONDON.

THE duke of Lancaster leads king Richard into London: they are met by the citizens.—The French author gives the following account of this meeting:

Quant il approche a 5 ou 6 mile pres de la ville de Londres, le maire, acompaigne de graut quantite de communes, ordonnez, & vestus chascun mestier, par son de divers draps, boyez & arivez vindrent a l'encontre de duc Henry; a grant quantite d'instrumens & de trompettes demenant, grant joie & grant consolacion.—Et la partoit on lespee devant la dit maire, comme devant le roy, a l'assemble le salurient, et le duc Henry apres, au qu'el ilz frent trop plus grant reverence qu'il n'avoient fait au roy, criant en leur language, d'une haute voix et espoventable, "Vive le bon duc de Lancastre!" Et disoit l'un a l'autre, "Que Dieux leur avoit monstre beau miracle, quant il leur avoit envoie le dit duc; et comment il avoit conquis tout le royaume d'Engleterre en moins d'un mops; et que bein devoit estre roy, qui ainsi s'avoit conquierir." Et en loient et gracioient notre Seigneur moult devotement, disant, "Que estoit sa voulente et que autrement, ne l'eust il peu avoir fait." Encores, disoient les foles et incredules gens, qu'il conquerroit une des grans parties du mond, et le comparoient desia a Alixandre le Grant. Ainsi disant et monopolant.—Approucherent de la ville sicomme a deux mile, et la s'arresta tout l'ost d'une partie & d'autre; lors dist le duc Henry, mult hault, aux communes de la dit ville, "Beaux seigneurs, very vetre roy! regardez que vous en volez faire." Et ils respondirent, a haute voix, "Nous volez qu'il soit mene & Westmonstre."—Et ainsi le duc Henry delivra son droit seigneur au turbe de Londres, afin telle que s'ils le faisoient mourir, qu'il peust dire, "Je sui innocent de ce fait icy."

—Ainsi emmenerent les comunes & le turbe de Londres leur roy a Westmonstre, et la duc tourna au tour de la ville.

In English:

"When they approached within 5 or 6 miles of the city of London, the mayor, accompanied with a great number of the common people, all in order, and habited every one according to his trade, with divers flags, came thus far to meet the duke Henry; with them they had many various instruments of music and trumpets, rejoicing exceedingly. And before the said mayor they carried a sword, in like manner as is done before the king. When the assembly were arrived they saluted the king,

king, and after him the duke Henry, to whom they paid a greater reverence than they had done to the king, crying aloud in their language, in a tumultous manner, " Long live the good duke of Lancaster!" And then they said one to another, " This is a fair miracle which God had shown to them, in sending the aforesaid duke; and how he had conquered all England in lefs than the space of one month; and that he ought surely to be king, who so well knew how to conquer." And then they thanked our Lord very devoutly, saying, " That it was his will that these things should be so, or else they could not have been done." And again, these foolish and credulous people said, that he had conquered a great part of the world, and compared him with Alexander the Great. In this manner talked they and boasted. —As they came near the city, at the distance of about two miles, all of them made a stop, as well one part as the other; and then duke Henry spake aloud to the common people of the said city, saying, " Good people, behold here your king! see what you will do with him." And they answered with loud voices, " We will have him led to Westminster."—And so duke Henry delivered his true lord to the common people and mob of London, that if in the end they should put him to death, he might say, " I am innocent of this deed."———

— And so the commons and mob of London conducted their king to Westminster, and the duke turned to the tower of the city."

The principal citizen is in pink, and his hose are green; the figure before him is in green, him behind in red, and the next to him in blue; the first (right hand) soldier is in a deep lead colour, the next in blue, and the third in lead colour; the first of the two that appear above is in pink and gold, and the next red and gold: the ground proper; the roof of the building is red, and the back ground blue and gold.

From the fame MS. as No. XX.

No. XXXII.

No. XXXII.

KING RICHARD RESIGNS HIS CROWN AND STATE.

This plate is copied from an illumination found in an old tranfcript of Froifart's chronicle, in the Royal Library, which feems, by the hand, to have been written towards the latter end of the reign of Henry the Sixth. The original is done with good tafte (confidering the poor flate of the art at that time) and is well finifhed. Great pains appears to have been taken with the faces in particular, which may juftly lead one to conclude that they were done from fomething of authority, though they are not quite fo ancient as the point of hiftory they are defigned to illuftrate.

The prefent plate before us reprefents king Richard the Second in his royal robes, refigning his crown and fcepter into the hands of Henry duke of Lancafter, who received them with much pretended diffidence and humility. The perfons prefent at this refignation were, Thomas Arundel, archbifhop of Canterbury; Richard Scrope, archbifhop of York; John, bifhop of Hereford; Henry, earl of Northumberland; Ralph Nevil, earl of Weftmorland; Thomas, lord Berkley; William, abbot of Weftminfter; John, prior of Canterbury; William Thyrning, Hugh Burnell, Thomas Erpingham, and Thomas Grey, knights; John Markham, juftice; Thomas Stow and John Burbage, doctors of civil law; Thomas Ferely and Denis Lopeham, public notaries.

This fcene was tranfacted at the king's lodgings, he being then a prifoner in the tower of London.—See a full account of the whole ceremony in Holingfhead's Chronicle.

This being the end of Lancafter's ambition, unfortunate Richard was deprived of his dignity, and fhortly after of his life. This prince was uncommonly imprudent in his conduct; however, he wanted not his flatterers.—The French author, to whom we are indebted for fo many of the foregoing plates, is very lavifh in his encomiums upon this unhappy man; and, after having defcribed his amiable qualities and accomplifhments, he mentions his genius for poetry, which I believe has efcaped all other hiftorians. His words are

Et si fais oit balades & chancons,
Rondeaulx & lais,
Ties bein & bel,——

" And he also made ballads and songs, rondeaus and poems, fairly and well."

The king's robe is a deep blue, and his close coat a deepish pink: Lancaster is in a deep pink: the figure behind him is in blue, with yellow sleeves and cape: that behind is in pink; and the man with a boot is in green, with red sleeves and blue hose; his boot is yellow, and his cap is green: the figure in front is in pink, blue hose and a red cap; and that behind has a blue cap, pink coat and red hose: both the figures with the rolls are in pink, sitting on green benches: the figure in the cowl (next the king) is in purple, and the next is in a dark blue loose coat and purple hose, with a green cap; the other figure (discoursing with him) is in red; and the figure in the door-way has on a pink coat and red hose. The whole of the room, throne, and the step, are green; the sky through the windows blue, and the canopy and hangings to the throne red and gold; the pavement is light and dark red; the crown, scepter, collars, &c. are gold.

The MS. from which this is taken, is marked 18 E. 2.

No. XXXIII.

THE PARLIAMENT IN WHICH LANCASTER WAS ELECTED KING.

A Representation of the parliament in which Richard's refignation of the crown was declared, and the duke of Lancafter recognized for king: the fpiritual lords fit on the right hand of the throne, the temporal lords (knights, &c.) on the left: Lancafter is in black behind.—Their particular perfons may be known from the following quotation from the author:

Anfi firent leur affamblee,
Qui eftoit de mal enpenfee,
A Wemonftre, hors la ville.

And afterwards,

Entour le dit fiege afes pres
Eftoient les prelas affis,
De quoy il y avoit plus de fis,
D'autre cofte toute les feigneurs,
Grans moyens peris et mencurs,
Affis par ordonnance belle,
Onequcs n'oy parler de telle:

Premiers feoit le duc Henry,
Et puis tout au plus pres de ly
Le duc Diore, fon beau coufin,
Qui n'avoit pas le cuer trop fin
Ters fon nepvou la roy Richart,
Apres, de cefte mefme part,
Le duc Daumarle fe feoit,
Qui fils a duc Diore eftoit;
Et puis le bon duc de Souldray,
Qui fu tonfiours loyal et vray.
Apres feoit le duc Dercestre,
Qui ne devoit pas faveur eftre,
Car il veoit devant ly faire
La paycil pour le roy deffaire,

Qui eftoit fon frere germain;
De ce fair au foin et au main
Avoient tous grant voulente.
Apres, eftoit de ce cofte,
Un autre, qui or non le marquis,
Seigneur eftoit de grant pris
Et puis, le conte D'arondel,
Qui eft affes june et pfuel,
Apres de Pointe le conte
De fu pas oublie ou compte
Aufti, ne fu eft de la Marche,
Apres yot d'une, autre Marche,
Un qui fu conte de Stanford,
Le quel n'aimoit pas la concorde
De fon feigneur le roy Richart.
Encor, feoit de cefte part,
Un qui fuoy afes nommee
Conte de Pancbrac et Ber;
Et tout au plus pres de cely
S'ift le conte de Salfebery,
Qui fu loyal jufqua la fin,
Quant ains le roy de cuer fin.
Le conte Dumeftal y fu,
Si comme je lay entendu,
Tous autres contes et feigneurs,
Et du royaume les greigneurs;
Eftoient a celle affemblee
Sians voulente et penfee

K   Deglife

Deslije la un autje rop,   Toute sour en effant sans soir,
La effoient, par bel avop,   Et pour miculx faije leur debair
Le route de Porthomberlant,   Sa genoilloient moult souvent;
Et le route de Westmerlant.   Je ne sap pourquop, ne comment.

In Englifh:

" And they made their evil-minded affembly at Weftminfter, without the city
—Round about near the throne fat the prelates, and on the other fide were all the
nobles of the land, from the greateft to the leaft, feated in juft order, as I fhall proceed to fhow:

Firft fat duke Henry, and clofe to him the duke of York, his coufin, whofe heart
was not faithful to his nephew Richard. After him, on the fame fide, fat the
duke of Aumarle, the fon of the duke of York; and alfo the good duke of Surrey,
who was always true and loyal. After him fat the duke of Exeter, who had no
caufe of joy, becaufe they were there making the neceffary preparations to dethrone
the king, who was his brother-in-law; for the people were all of them refolved
upon this act. After him, on the fame fide, fat another who bore the name of
marquis, a lord of great poffeffion alfo, the earl of Arundel, a fair young man.
After him the earl of Norwich ought not to be forgot, nor him of March.
Befides thefe, there was another called the earl of Stamford, who fought not the
peace of his lord king Richard. Again, upon that fame fide, I ought to name
the earl of Pembroke and Bury; and clofe to him fat the earl of Salifbury, who
was loyal to the laft, and loved the king with a faithful heart. The earl of Dun-
ftable was alfo there, as I heard, as well as all the other earls and lords; the chief
of the realm; and they were met in this affembly with the thought and defire to
fet up another king.—With them, and moved by the fame defire, was the earl of
Northumberland, and the earl of Weftmorland. Thefe two continued all the time
without being feated, and, the better to exprefs their duty, were often kneeling; but
I know not in what manner, or to what purpofe."——The bifhops are not named.

The throne is red and gold; Lancafter as before in No. XXXI. The
figure next him is all in gold; the next to him is in blue, and a brown cap;
and the next red and gold flowers, with a blue cap; the next in purple and
gold, and a green cap and red feet: the ftep is blue. The earl of Northumberland (ftanding on the right) is in blue and gold, lined with white,
and red fleeves; the earl of Weftmorland (on the left) is in green. The
bifhop next the throne is in black, and a brown cowl; the next fky blue;
the next deep blue; the next red; and the next deep blue again; and the
part that appears of another figure is pink. The roof on the top is red, and
back ground to it blue flowered with gold. The building is of a lead colour, and the ceiling blue.

This is from the fame MS. as No. XX.

7   I here

XXXIV

ANTIQUITIES OF ENGLAND. 67

I HERE take the liberty to break into the regular feries of monarchs and hiftorical facts, to introduce fome few interefting portraits of great perfonages, who flourifhed in fome of the foregoing reigns. Moft of them are from the catalogue of benefactors to the abbey of St. Alban's *; which catalogue feems to have been begun by the monks there, about the latter end of the reign of Richard the Second, and was finifhed in the life-time of king Henry the Sixth.—In it are preferved many well-finifhed portraits of the charitable contributors to the above abbey.

A great many of the illuminations in this MS. were drawn by the hand of ALAN STRAYLER, who it feems was a defigner and painter.—Weever fpeaks of him as follows:

" I had like to have forgotten Alan Strayler, the painter or limner out of pictures, in the Golden Regifter," [the MS. above mentioned was fo called] " of all the benefactours to this abbey; who, for fuch his paines (howfoever he was well payed) and for that he forgave three fhillings fourpence of an old debt owing unto him for colours, is thus remembered :

   Nomen pictoris Alanus Strayler, habetur
   Qui fine fine choris celeftibus affocietur."

· " The painter's name is Alan Strayler, who fhall be received as a companion of the heavenly choir for ever †."

In the MS. itfelf, the portrait of this painter occurs with the mention made of his forgiving the debt, as declared above, as well as thefe verfes.

No. XXXIV.
QUEEN MATILDA

Is the portrait of " Matilbis Regina," the pious queen, firft wife to king Henry the Firft, who in her youth was brought up in a monaftic way of life, and on her advancement beftowed feveral liberal donations on many abbeys, convents, &c. She was daughter to Malcolme the Third, king of

---
 * This book is in the Cotton library, and is marked Nero, D. VII.
 † Ancient Funeral Monuments, page 578.

K 2   Scotland :

Scotland: her mother was Margaret, daughter to Edward, the son of Edmund Ironsides, king of England.—Holingshead gives the following account of this Matilda:

" And ere long they considered how Edgar, king of Scotland, had a sister named Maud, a beautiful lady and of virtuous conditions, who was a professed nun in a religious house, to the end she might avoid the storms of the world, and lead her life in more security, after her father's decease. This woman, notwithstanding her vow, was thought to be a meet bedfellow for the king; therefore he sent ambassadors to her brother Edgar, requiring him that he might have her in marriage. But she refusing superstitiously at the first to break her profession or vow, would not hear of the offer: wherewithal king Henry being the more enflamed, sendeth new embassadors, to move the same in more earnest sort than before; insomuch that Edgar, upon the declaration of their embassy, set the abbess of the house wherein she was enclosed, in hand to persuade her to the marriage, the which so effectually declared unto her, in sundry wise, how necessary, profitable and honourable this same should be, both to her country and kindred, did so prevail at last, that the young lady granted willingly to the marriage.— Hereupon she was conveyed into England, and married to the king, who caused the archbishop Anselm to crown her queen, on saint Martin's day, which fell, as that year come about, upon the Sunday, being the eleventh of November, A. D. 1100."

Her close dress is a very dark pink; and her robe a deep red, lined with white, cross'd with pink; her head-dress is white, and a gold crown: the cushion to the seat is red, the seat stone-colour; the back ground light yellow, flowered with purple, and the frame a deep purple.

No. XXXV.

XXXV

No. XXXV.

JOAN, PRINCESS OF WALES.

This plate represents Joan, countess of Kent, who was the wife of Edward the Black Prince, and married to him in the year 1361.

Speed gives us the following account:

" Edward, the eldest son of king Edward the Third, and born at Woodstock, July 15, the 3d year of his father's reign, A. D. 1329, was created prince of Wales, duke of Aquitaine and Cornwall, and earl of Chester: he was also earl of Kent in right of this lady, who was the most admired lady of that age, daughter of Edmond earl of Kent, brother by the father's side to king Edward the Second. She had been twice married before; first, to the valiant earl of Salisbury, from whom she was divorced; next, to the lord Thomas Holland; after whose decease, this prince, passionately loving her, did marry her. By her he had issue two sons: Edward, the eldest, born at Angolesme, who died at seven years of age; and Richard, born at Bourdeaux, who after his father's death was prince of Wales, and after the death of his grandfather (king Edward the Third) king of England."

The present portrait, which is the only one of this princess that I have found, is extremely well finished. She holds in her hand the box of gold which she gave to the abbey. Her dress is very curious, though nothing can be said in praise of its elegance.

Her close dress is cloth of gold flowered, with red ornaments. The robe which comes over her shoulders, and also falls down, covering her knees, is red, enriched with purple flowers; this robe is lined with ermine. The
box

box is gold, which she holds in her left hand. Her head-drefs appears to be a pure white; and the three parts of an under veil which is seen hanging over her forehead and cheeks, is like a fine lawn. Her seat is of a stone colour; the back ground is dark and light blue, flowered; and the frame which encompasses the whole is red and white.

XXXVI

ANTIQUITIES OF ENGLAND.

No. XXXVI.

CONSTANCE, QUEEN OF CASTILE.

THE firſt of the two portraits repreſented on this plate is Conſtance, eldeſt daughter of Peter, king of Caſtile and Leon. She was married A. D. 1372, to John of Gaunt, duke of Lancaſter (fourth ſon of Edward the Third) who, in right of his wife, took upon him the title of "KING OF CASTILE AND LEON." She died A. D. 1394.

Holingſhead writes as follows:

" In this xlvi. yeare, the duke of Lancaſter, being as then a widower, married the lady Conſtance, eldeſt daughter to Peter king of Spaine, which was ſlayne by the baſtarde brother Henrie (as before ye have heard).

" Alſo the lorde Edmonde, earle of Cambridge, married the ladye Iſabell, ſiſter to the ſame Conſtance. Their other ſiſter, named Beatrice, affianced to Don Ferdinando, ſonne to Peter king of Portingale, was departed this life a little before this tyme, at Bayonne, where they were all three left as hoſtages by theyr father, when the prince went to bring him home into his country (as before ye may reade).

" Froiſſart writeth, that the duke married the ladie Conſtance in Gaſcoigne, and that ſhortly after he returned into England with his ſayde wife, and hir ſiſter, leaving the Capital de Bueffz, and other lordes of Gaſcoigne and Poiƈtou, in charge with the rule of thoſe countrys. By reaſon of that marriage, the duke of Lancaſter, as in right of his wife, being the elder ſiſter, cauſed himſelf to be intituled king of Caſtile, and his ſayde wife queene of the ſame realme."

MARGARET, DUCHESS OF NORFOLK.

THE ſecond portrait is Margaret, ducheſs of Norfolk, daughter to Thomas of Brotherton, fifth ſon of Edward the Firſt. She was twice married. Her firſt huſband was John lord Segrave, who died in the 27th year of

Edward

REGAL AND ECCLESIASTICAL

Edward the Third ; by whom she had no issue. Then she was re-married to her second husband, Sir Walter Manny, knight of the garter, lord of the town of Manny, in the diocese of Cambray : him she also out-lived, and died the 24th of March, in the first year of Henry the Fourth. She put in her claim to the marshalship of England, at the coronation of Richard the Second. (See page 32.)

The close dress of Constance is a deep red bound with gold, and a white bracelet on her arm; the garment she holds up is a crimson red; her head-dress is white, and the four balls are gold : the back ground blue, white, and gold ; the frame blue, the corners gold, and the purse white.

The robe and head dress of the duchess of Norfolk are white; the purse is gold; the back ground blue, white and gold; and the frame red, with gold corners.

XXXVII

ANTIQUITIES OF ENGLAND.

No. XXXVII.

CHAUCER.

THIS portrait of Chaucer is preferved in a book written by his difciple OCCLEVE, or HOCCLEVE, who was fome time keeper of the privy fignet office *. He, out of love and refpect to his dead mafter, caufed this portrait to be done, which is pointing to thefe lines:

> And though his lyfe be quepnt, the refemblaunce
> Of him in me hath fo frefhe lyffynesse,
> That to putte othje men in remembjaunce
> Of his perfone, I have heere his lyknesse
> Soo made to this end, in foth faftnesse,
> That thei that have of him left thought and mynde,
> By this peynture may ageyn him fynde,

Chaucer is often called, by our Englifh hiftorians, the Prince of Poets. His parents are not known; yet certain it is, that he was in great efteem at court in the reign of Edward the Third, &c. and his works are, even now, much refpected, notwithftanding their homely ftile and obfolete terms, through which moft of their antient beauty is loft. He was married to the daughter of Payne Roet, knight, and died A. D. 1400, ætat. fui 70 †.

Take alfo the following lines written by the fame Hocceleve in praife of Chaucer, his deceafed mafter. This is extracted from his poem, intituled "De Regimine Principis."

> But welaway, fo is mine hajt woe,
> That the honour of Englifh tongue is deed,
> Of which I wont was counfaile have and reed.
> O mafter deje, and fadje revejent!
> My mafter Chaucer, flowje of eloquence,
> Mijjor of fructuous entendement;
> O univerfall fadje of fcience!
> Alafs! that thou thine excellent prudence

---

* This MS. is preferved in the Harleian library, marked 4866.
† Granger Biog. Hift.

In thy bed mortal mightest not bequeath.
What eyld Death? Alas! why would she the fle?
O Death, that didest not harme singler in slaughter of him,
But all the land smerteth!
But natheleffe, yet hast thou no power his name fle;
His hie vertue affecteth
Unslaine fro thee, which ay us lifely herteth,
With bookes of his own ornat enditing,
That is to all this land enlumining.

The figure is in a dark lead-coloured garment, and the back ground is green.

No. XXXVIII.

CORONATION OF HENRY THE FOURTH.

Tʜɪs plate reprefents the coronation of king Henry the Fourth, which ceremony was performed by Thomas Arundel, archbifhop of Canterbury, and Richard Scrope, archbifhop of York, at Weftminfter. It is great pity that the reft of the attendants (which doubtlefs are likeneffes of many of the principal perfonages of the realm) fhould, for want of a proper defcription (by the author) be loft to the world. The figure kneeling in front, perhaps, may be defigned to reprefent the abbot of Weftminfter, holding the great miffal book, while the archbifhop performs the facred fervice.

" In the morrow (fays Holingfhead) being faint George's day, and 13th of October, A. D. 1399, the lord mayor of London road towards the Tower to attend the king, with diverfe worfhipfull citizens clothed all in red; and from the Tower the king ridde through the citie unto Weftminfter, where he was facred, annoynted, and crowned king, by the archbifhop of Canterburie, with all the ceremonies and royall folemnitie as was due and requifite.

" And at the day of his coronation (as fayth Hall) becaufe he would not have it thought that he took upon him the crowne without good title and right therunto had, therefore he caufed it to be proclaymed and publifhed, that he challenged the realme not only by conqueft, but alfo that he was by king Richard adopted as heyre, and declared fucceffor of hym, and by refignation had accepted the crowne and fcepter ; and alfo that he was next heire male of the blood royall to king Richarde.

" Though all other rejoyced at his advancement, yet furely Edmonde Mortimer, earle of March, which was coufin and heyre to Lionell duke of Clarence, the third begotten fonne of king Edward the Third, and Richard earle of Cambridge, fonne to Edmonde duke of York, which he had married Anne, fifter to the fame Edmonde, where with thefe doings neither pleafed nor contented ; infomuch that now the devifon once begon, the one linage ceaffed not to perfecute the other, till the heyres males of both the lynes were clearly deftroyed and extinct."

REGAL AND ECCLESIASTICAL

The king's robe is blue, and his clofe coat purple. The archbifhop on his right hand is in red, bordered with gold, and a white clofe garment; his mitre is white, ftriped and flowered with gold. The other archbifhop is in deep pink, and white fleeves and gloves. The figure next him is in purple, and the other figure between them red; both have green caps. The herald is counter-changed, blue and red; his armour black and white. The figure kneeling is in light green, holding a red book: the part of a figure behind the column (to the right) is in red, and a purple cap; the firft whole figure purple, and a blue cap; the next blue, and a purple cap; and the figure between them is red, and has a green cap. The front figure on the other fide is in pink, and a blue cap; and the figure behind him is in blue. The throne behind is blue and gold, and the ftep and pavement green, as is all the back ground: the fky is blue; the columns are light blue, topp'd with ftone colour.

This plate is taken from a curious MS. of Froiffart's chronicle, an account of which is given under No. XXXII. this plate being alfo from the fame book, and marked 18 E. 2.

XXXIX

No. XXXIX.

KING HENRY THE FOURTH AND HIS COURT.

The valuable original of this plate is preserved in a large folio book, intituled "Regimine Principis," which was translated from the Latin by Hoccleve, the disciple of Geofry Chaucer, as is supposed at the command of king Henry the Fourth. There is also bound up in the same volume, another book, written in a hand of the same date, and very like each other, intituled "Vigestus de re militari," the conclusion of which MS. is thus set forth in old English:

Here endeth the book that clepkes clepnin, in Latyne, Vigestus de re militari; we, of Vigestus of debus of knyghtes. The whiche book was translated and turned from Latyn into Englishe, at the ordonnance and byddynge of the worthie worshepful lord Sire Thomas of Berkeley, to gret dispozt and dalpaunce of lordes and alle worthie wexpionrs, that ben apassed by wey of age al labour and travailling, and to grete information and serbing of yonge lordes and knyghtes, that ben lusty, and loves to here and see and to use debus of aymes and chibalrye℄: —The turnpnge of this book into Englishe, was wretten and ended in vigile of Al-halewes, the yeat of our Lord a thousand four hundred and eighte, the X year of king Henry the Forthe: To him and to us alle God graunt grace of our offendynge, space to our amendynge, and his face to seen at oure endyng: Amen, —This is is name that turned this book from Latyn into Englishe,

Worshepful ▢ tonn.

Which emblematical figure I must own I cannot at all explain, but without doubt it is meant to express the name of the translator.

As the hands of these two different MSS. do so well agree, and this last is thus dated, there is not much doubt to be made of the first being written nearly at the same time; if so, it is most likely that it was not only done while Hoccleve lived, but that it was also the present book given to the king, which seems to be confirmed by the illumination. The king is here represented habited in his royal robes, in presence of his court, receiving the book presented to him by Hoccleve, who is kneeling before him: but still

REGAL AND ECCLESIASTICAL

ftill here we meet with the fame unhappy difficulty, in not being able to determine who the particular attendant perfons are.

This book is in the Bodleian library at Oxford *.

The king fits on a throne of gold fhadowed with red; his robe is blue, lined with ermine; and the figure kneeling is in a dark lead colour: the perfon next him is in red, and the cape of his cloke is blue and gold; the cap red, ornamented with a precious ftone: the next figure is in white and blue, a black girdle ftudded with gold, hat and hofe of a dark lead colour. The firft of the three figures to the right is in light pink, blue mantle and a white cape, black cap and fhoes, and white gloves; the middle figure is in a very dark-coloured garment, girdle ftudded with gold, and blue hat; the laft figure is in white and pink, gold ftudded girdle, and a reddifh-coloured hood. The back ground is red and gold.

* It is marked Digby, 233.

No. XL.

HENRY THE FIFTH.

THE illumination from which this plate is copied, is in a book written in old French, preferved in the library of Bennet (otherwife CORPUS CHRISTI) college, Cambridge. The book itfelf is a tranflation of cardinal Bonaventura's Life of Chrift, made by John de Galopes, dean of the collegiate church of St. Louis in Normandy.

I here take the liberty of thanking the Reverend Mr. Tyfon, fellow of the above college, to whom I am obliged not only for the pointing out, and procuring me the ufe of, this valuable MS. but alfo for the trouble he took in fhewing me whatever he thought might be curious, or ufeful to my undertaking, during my ftay at that Univerfity. This ingenious gentleman, among feveral other curious works, etched an outline of this very illumination, and printed a concife account of it, to prefent to his friends; from which I have borrowed the following intelligence:

" The picture reprefents John de Galopes, the tranflator, offering his book, covered with crimfon velvet, to that moft glorious prince, king Henry the fifth, who is feated on his throne, which is blue fringed with gold, and powdered with the gold text letter S. This (Mr. Tyfon conceives) may perhaps mean SOVERAYNE, as that word appears frequently on the tomb of his father at Canterbury. On the king's right hand ftand two ecclefiaftics: he on the fore-ground holds in his hand a black cap, called MORTIER by the French, and always worn by their chancellors and prefidents à mortier."

Then Mr. Tyfon tells us, that a learned friend of his fufpects it may be the famous cardinal Lewis de Luxemburgh, chancellor of France and bifhop of Terounne, afterwards archbifhop of Rouen, and perpetual adminiftrator of the diocefe of Ely. He died at Hatfield, September the 18th, 1443.

Among feveral proofs offered by this learned gentleman of the genuinenefs of the portrait, thefe feem to be very ftriking ones. Firft, that the difpofition of the figures, the drawing and the colouring of this miniature,

all

all shew the hand of an able artist. Next it appears that the book, in which this illumination is preserved, was originally presented to the king himself, and was afterwards his property.—" This (continues my author) is another mark of the resemblance being genuine; for it cannot be supposed that the author would have presented the king with so laboured a miniature of his Majesty, if he had not been able to procure a real likeness."

At the end of the book, in a round hand, of the time of Henry the Eighth, or queen Elizabeth, is written this entry:

This waſſe ſumtyme kinge Henri the Fifeth his booke; which conteineth the lyfe of Chriſt, &c. the pſalmes of the patriarches and prophetes; the pſalmes of the prophet David omittid.

Sani excilent notes, thoughe ſome thinges, waienge the tyme, may be amendid. Rede, iudge, and thank God for a better light.

The king's robe is crimson, lined with white; his collar is gold, and his girdle is of the same; his leg is black, with the garter gold. The two ecclesiastics are in a lightish pink. The officer holding the mace is in a short green coat; one leg is red and the other white. John de Galopes is in light purple, and the book is crimson. The throne is blue, powdered with the gold letter S. The back ground is blue and gold; and the pavement is chequer-work of green, yellow, black and white.

ANTIQUITIES OF ENGLAND.

No. XLI.

KING HENRY THE SIXTH AND HIS PARLIAMENT AT BURY.

REPRESENTS WILLIAM CURTEIS, abbot of St. Edmund's-Bury abbey, prefenting to king Henry the Sixth a book tranflated out of the Latin, by John Lidgate, a monk there, which the king receives feated on his throne, furrounded by his court : this was tranfacted at Bury, while the king held his Chriftmas there. It is very likely that the two figures, one on the king's left hand, and the other behind the fword-bearer, who are both of them covered, are the king's two uncles, John Duke of Bedford, regent of France, and Humphry duke of Glocefter, third and fourth fons of Henry the Fourth.

This book * contains the life of St. Edmund, king of the Eaft Angles, and is illuftrated with many beautiful pictures, reprefenting the principal accidents of the hiftory. At the beginning is Lidgate's prologue, which runs thus :

   When I firſt gan on this tranſlation,
   It was the pere by computacion,
   When fixte Henry, in his eſtat roial,
   With his feeptre of England and of France,
   Hield at Bury the feſte pzincipal
   Of Chriſtemeſſe, with full gret habundance;
   And after that lift to have plefance,
   As his confail gan for him provide
   There in this place till Heſterne for to abide.

And then he goes on,

   In this mater there is no moze to feyn,
   Sauf to the kyng for to do plefance,
   Th' abbot William, his humble chapeleyn,
   Gaf me in chazge to do myn attendance.
   The noble ſtozy to tranſlate in fubſtance

---

* This book is preferved in the Harleian Library, and is marked 2278.

REGAL AND ECCLESIASTICAL

Out of latyn, aftir my kunnyng,
The in ful purpose to gibe it to the kyng.

And this appears to be the very book which was prefented to the king [*].

The king's robe is a light brown, and his clofe coat is gold : he is feated on a throne of light grey, with a dark pink canopy. The firft figure, on his left hand, is entirely dreffed in gold; the next in a light brown, with white flowers, edged with gold, and a deep pink cap. The fword-bearer is in dark brown, with light flowers : the figure behind him is entirely in gold, with a pink cap; and the figure befide him is in a light pink. All the ecclefiaftics are in black. The feven figures at the bottom are in a white, fhaded with a dirty pink. The book prefented to the king, is red; the other, held by the monk, gold; and that on the ftand in front, blue : the ftand is brown, and the candlefticks are gold. The pavement is light and dark green; the building that furrounds them is brown, and the fky a deep blue. The frame is light and dark pink.

[*] See the Harleian Catalogue, No. 2278.

No. XLII.

XLI

No. XLII.

KING HENRY THE SIXTH, AND LIDGATE.

THIS is from a MS. in the Bodleian library, Oxford, and reprefents John Lidgate, the author, prefenting it to king Henry the Sixth*. The perfon ftanding by the king is, without doubt, either one of the king's uncles, or fome other great lord of the court. The crown, or coronet, differs much from that of the king's, and is perhaps the ducal coronet.

This prince, though a juft, pious and worthy man, was very unfortunate in this life, bandied about by the fudden gufts of cruel fortune, and the ambitious defigns of artful men. Thefe mifchances were, perhaps, fomewhat owing to the daring and turbulent difpofition of his queen.—The characters of this prince and his confort are given below from Grafton; and they are juftly drawn, though in a very homely phrafe:

" King Henry, which raigned at this time, was a man of a meek fpirit and of a fimple witte, prefering peace before warre, reft before bufineffe, honeftie before profite, and quietnefs before laboure : and to the intent that men might perceive that there could be none more chafte, more meek, more holye, nor a better creature, in him raigned fhamefafedneſs, modeftie, integritie, and pacience to be marveylled at, taking and fuffering all loffes, chaunces, difpleafures, and fuch worldly tormentes, in good parte, and wyth a pacient manner, as though they had chaunced by his own faulte, or negligent overfight ; and he was governed of them whom he fhould have ruled, and brideled of fuch whom he fharply fhould have fpurred: he gaped not for honour, nor thurfted for riches, but ftudied onlye for the health of his foule, the faving wherof he efteemed to be the greateft wifdome, and the loffe thereof the extremeft folie, that could be. But, on the other part, the queen Margaret of Anjou was a woman of great witte, and yet of no greater witte than of haute ftomache, defirous of glorie, and covetous of honour ; and of reafon, pollicye, counfaill, and other giftes

* This book is marked Digby, 233, Bib. Bod.

and talantes of nature, fhe lacked nothing, nor of diligence, ftudie, and bufineffe, fhe was not unexpert: but yet fhe had one pointe of a very woman; for oftentimes, when fhe was vehement and fully bent in a matter, fhe was fodainely like to the weather-cocke mutable and turning. This woman, perceyving that her hufband did not frankly rule as he would, but did all things by the advice and counfaile of Humfrey duke of Gloucefter, and that he paffed not much on the authoritye and governaunce of the realme, determined with herfelf to take uppon her the rule and regiment both of the king and his kingdome, and to deprive and remove out of all rule and audthoritye the fayde duke, then called the lord proteƊour of the realme; leaft men fhoulde fay and report, that fhe had neither wit nor ftomack, which would permit and fuffer her hufband, being of perfite age and man's eftate, like a young fcholar, or innocent pupile, to be governed by the difpofition of another man."

I take this opportunity of expreffing my acknowledgments of the favours I received at the hands of Dr. Bever, of All Souls, and the Rev. Mr. Price, mafter of the Bodleian Library, who kindly procured me the ufe of this and the foregoing MS. and alfo for the pains they jointly took in fhewing me whatever they thought worthy notice, while I was at Oxford.

The throne is red, ftriped with gold: the king's robe is blue, lined with ermine; the under garment and gloves are red: the officer on his right is in green and red, his hofe red with filver ftripes; the figure to the left is in green and red, and a green coronet; all having golden girdles. Lidgate is in black, prefenting the book, edged with gold. The back ground is red ftriped with gold, and the frame blue and white.

No. XLIII.

No. XLIII.

HENRY THE SIXTH, AND HIS COURT.

THE valuable picture here copied is in a large folio MS. most elegantly written and illuminated; it contains, among several romances and other matters, an account of the order of the garter*. It was written at the command of John Talbot, earl of Shrewsbury; and this illumination represents him in his habit of the garter, presenting the book to Margaret of Anjou, queen to king Henry the Sixth, who, together with the king, is seated on a rich throne, surrounded by the lords and ladies of the court. On the king's right hand stand two figures, one having a coronet on his head, and the other a plain hoop or circle of gold. The figure with the coronet, I take it, is designed for the king's uncle, Humphry duke of Glocester, because it much resembles the illumination copied at the bottom of the following plate, which is certainly designed for him. This portrait of the earl of Shrewsbury is said to agree exactly with an old painting of him, that is to be seen at the Herald's office.

" In the year 1441, (says Holingshead) John, the valiant lord Talbot, for his approved prowess and tried valour, shewed in the French wars, was created earl of Shrewesbury, and, with a company of three thousand men, sente agayne into Normandye, for the better defence of the same."

And a little after, the same author relates the manner of the earl's death as follows:

" The Frenchmen that lay before the town of Chastilon, hearing by their scouts that the erle of Shrowsbury advanced with his troops, left the seige, and retired in good order into a place whiche they hadde trenched, diched, and fortified with oridinance.

" The erle, advertized how the siege was removed, hasted forward towardes his enemies, doubting most least they woulde have bin quite fled and gone before his comming: but they, fearing the displeasure of the French king (who was not far off) if they should have fled, abode the erle's

---

* This is marked 15 E. 6. and is preserved in the Royal Library.

comming, and fo received him, that though he firſte with manfull courage and ſo fighting wanne the entry of their camp, yet at length they compaſſed him about, and ſhooting him throughe the thighe with an hand gunne, ſlew his horſe, and finally killed him, lying on the ground, whom they durſt never look in the face while he ſtood on his feet.

" It is ſaid, that after he perceived there was no remidie, but the preſent loſs of the battle, he councilled his ſone, the lord Liſle, to ſave himſelf by flight, ſith the ſame could not redound to any great reproach in him, this being the firſt journey in which he had been preſent. Many words he uſed to have perſuaded him to ſave his life; but nature ſo wrought in the ſon, that neither deſire of life or fear of death could either cauſe him to ſhrink, or convey himſelf out of danger; and ſo there manfully he ended his life with his ſayde father, &c. &c."

The king's robe is blue, lined with ermine; the ſleeves of his coat are pink. The robe of the queen is a deep lake colour, with ſleeves of gold cloth, and a white ſtomacher. The ſeat is gold, and the ſtep it ſtands upon a darkiſh ſtone colour: the arms behind the throne, proper. The firſt of the two women behind the queen is dreſſed in gold, and her head-dreſs is pink and gold; and the ſecond is in blue, as is her head-dreſs: the crown'd figure beſide the king is in deep pink, turned up with green furring. The earl himſelf is in deep pink, lined with green; the garters are a light blue, and gold letters; the book is a deep red, and the claſps are gold; the dog behind the earl is white. The figure on the right hand, holding a mace, is in blue, with a reddiſh faſh, and his coat turn'd up with green furr, red hoſe, and black ſhoes: the figure behind is in red and a pink cap ornamented with a gold ſtar; the figure with his hand on his breaſt, next the mace-bearer, is in a pink coat furred with black, and black hoſe; and the next to him is in green, with red hoſe. The building is ſtone colour; the hangings red, ornamented with gold; and the pavement green and gold.

No. XLIV.

XLIV

No. XLIV*.

THOMAS BEAUCHAMP, EARL OF WARWICK, &c.
AND HUMPHRY, DUKE OF GLOCESTER, &c.

THE two figures on the top of this plate are the portraits of Thomas Beauchamp, earl of Warwick, and Margaret his wife. This Thomas was father to the great Richard Beauchamp, earl of Warwick, the glorious warrior in the reigns of Henry the Fifth and Henry the Sixth.

The bottom figures are Humphry duke of Glocefter, fourth fon of Henry the Fourth, and Eleanor Cobham, his fecond wife: fhe was daughter of Reginald lord Cobham, of Scarborough. She was accufed of witchcraft, and put to folemn penance for three feveral days at London, and was afterwards imprifoned in the Ifle of Man for life. Her hufband, the duke of Glocefter, was fhortly after arrefted for high treafon, and bafely murdered without any trial.

Speed gives the following concife account of the duke of Glocefter:

" Humfrey, the fourth fon of Henry the Fourth, was by his brother, king Henry the Fifth, created duke of Gloucefter, was protectour of the kingdome of Englande, for 25 years, in the time of king Henry the Sixt, in whofe firft yeare he ftiled himfelf in his charters thus: Humfrey, by the grace of God, fonne, brother, and uncle, to kings, duke of Gloucefter, earle of Henault, Holland, Zeland, and Pembroke, lord of Friefland, great chamberlaine of the kingdome of England, protectour and defender of the fame kingdome and church of England. He was a man who nobly deferv'd of the common-wealth, and of learning, as being himfelfe very learned, and a magnificent patron and benefactor to the univerfitie of Oxford, where he had been educated; and was generally called the good duke. He married firft, Jacoba, heir to William duke of Bavaria, earle of Holland, who (as was after known) had firft beene lawfully troth-plighted to John duke of Brabant, and therefore was afterward divorced from the faid

---

* This is from Nero, D. VII.—Vide page 67 of this book.

Humfrey.

Humfrey. His fecond wife was Elianor, daughter to Reginauld, baron* Cobham de Scarborough. Queen Margaret, wife to king Henry the Sixt, repining at his great power in fwaying the king, and fecretly wroughte his ruine, he being murthered in his bed at Burie, dying without any iffue, 1446. His body was buried at Saint Alban's; yet the vulgar error is, that he lies buried in Saint Paul's."

Both the top figures are dreffed in deep red; the woman's head-drefs is purple, gold, and white linen: the trees and ground proper; the back ground gold, and the frame blue.

The duchefs is habited in a reddifh pink gown: of the fame colour is the duke's robe and cap; his clofe coat is blue, and the lining of the robe is ermine. The head-drefs of the duchefs is black, and a gold coronet. The back ground is blue, flowered with gold, the pavement light and dark red, the frame red and gold.

No. XLV.

No. XLV.

THE EARL OF SALISBURY, AND LIDGATE.

This plate is from an old drawing (entirely of one colour, brown-like bister) contained in a MS. book in the Harleian Library*, the title of which is THE PILGRIM: it was written by John Lidgate, and the drawing represents the author presenting the book to Thomas Montacute, earl of Salisbury. The designer has enigmatically pictured the title of the book, in making the figure of a Pilgrim jointly holding and presenting it with Lidgate to the earl.

This noble warrior is very properly pictured in his armour, and his portrait is truly interesting, when we consider the consequence of his actions in France, during the wars carried on there in the reign of Henry the Sixth. He lost his life at the siege of Orleance; and the manner of his death is thus related by Holingshead:

" In the tower that was taken at the bridge ende, there was an high chamber, having a grate full of barres of yron, by the whiche a man myghte looke all the length of the bridge into the citie; at which grate many of the chiefe captaines stoode manie times, viewing the citie, and devising in what place it were best to give the assault. They within the citie well perceived thys peeping hole, and layde a piece of ordinance directly against the windowe.

" It so chanced, the 59 day after the siege was layde, the earle of Salisburie, Sir Thomas Gargrave, and William Glafsdale, with divers other, went into the saide tower, and so into the high chamber, and looked out at the grate; and within a short space, the sonne of the master gunner perceiving men looking out at the window, tooke his match, as his father had taught him, who was gone downe to dinner, and fired the gunne, the shot whereof brake and sheevered the iron barres of the grate, so that one of the same barres strake the earle so violently on the heade, that it stroke away one of his eyes and the syde of his cheeke.

" Sir Thomas Gargrave was likewise stricken, and dyed within two days.

* Marked 4826.

" The

"The earle was conveyed to Meun on Loire, where, after eight dayes, he likewife departed this worlde, whofe body was conveyed to England with all funerall pomp, and buried at Biffam by his progenitors, leaving behind him an only daughter, named Alice, married to Richard Nevill, fonne to Raufe earle of Weftmerlande.

"The domage that the realme of Englande receyved by the loffe of thys noble man, manifeftly appeared, in that immediately after hys death, the profperous good lucke whiche had followed the Englifh nation began to decline, and the glory of their victories, gotten in the parties beyond the fea, fell in decay.

"Though al men were forowful for his death, yet the duke of Bedford was moft ftriken with heavineffe, as he that had loft his only right hand and chiefe ayde in time of neceffitie."

XLVI

No. XLVI.

KING EDWARD THE FOURTH.

THIS plate is done from a valuable MS. in the Royal Library*, containing the chronicle of England, from Brute to the reign of Edward the Second: it was written at the command of Edward the Fourth, by the person who is kneeling before the king, and presenting the book. The king sits on his throne of state, richly habited, having on his head a blue velvet cap turned up with fine linen, instead of a crown. The figure on the left hand, with the insignia of the garter, may perhaps be intended for Richard duke of Gloucester, the king's brother.

A short sketch of the person and character of this king may not be unpleasing to the reader, which is set down as follows in Speed's Chronicle:

" Of personage he was the goodliest gentleman (faith Comines) that ever mine eyes beheld; faire of complexion, and of most princely presence, courageous of heart, politique in counsell: in adversitie, nothing abash'd; in prosperitie, rather joyous than proud: in peace, just and mercifull; in war sharpe and fierce, and in field bold and venturous, yet no further than wisedome would, and is no lesse commended where he avoided, then is his manhood when he vanquish'd: eight or nine battles he won, wherin, to his greater renowne, he fought on foote, and was ever victor over his enemies. Much given he was to the lusts of youth, and in his latter time growne somewhat corpulent, which rather adorned his graver yeeres, than any waies disliked the eyes of his beholders."

The king's robe is blue, powdered with golden lions intermixed with flower de luces; his cap is white fringed with gold; his neckcloth is white and a gold collar. The author is in a bright pink, and a black hood and girdle. The whole length figure, behind the author, is in a bright brown, deep purple sleeves, a gold collar, and blue cap: the figure he talks to is

* Marked 15 E 4.

in light red, and a brown cap and gold collar. The corner figure to the left is in a clear green, wearing a red cap, and a collar of gold about his neck, and in his hand he holds a gilt rod. The next figure is in deep crimſon, furred with very deep red, and ſleeves of the ſame; he alſo wears a red cap, and holds a golden wand; his collar and garter are gold, his legs blue, and black ſhoes. The throne is a clear brown, the back crimſon, and the curtains and canopy pink: the walls are green, and the arras is of a deep reddiſh brown flower'd with gold: the pavement is a ſtone colour.

XLVII

No. XLVII.

EDWARD THE FOURTH, HIS QUEEN AND SON, &c.

Is taken from a small folio MS. on vellum, in the archbishop's library at Lambeth*. It represents Anthony Woodville, earl of Rivers, presenting the book, and Caxton his printer, to king Edward the Fourth, the queen and prince. The portrait of the prince (afterwards Edward the Fifth) is the only one known of him, and has been engraved by Vertue among the heads of the kings. The person in a cap and robe of state is, probably, Richard duke of Gloucester, as he resembles the king, and as Clarence was always too great an enemy of the queen to be distinguished by her brother. The book was printed in 1477, when Clarence was in Ireland, and in the beginning of the next year he was murdered. At the end of the MS. is this curious monagram:

/·TER/

See a further account of this book in the Hon. Mr. Walpole's Catalogue of the Royal and Noble Authors, page 52; and in Ames's History of Printing, page 9.

" The queen of Edward the Fourth (says Speed) was Elizabeth, the daughter of Richard Woodvill, earl Rivers, by his wife Jaquelana dutchesse of Bedford (who was the daughter of Peter earl of Saint Paul, and hee the sonne of Peter de Luxemburgh); was first married unto Sir John Grey, slaine at Saint Alban's, where he was knighted the daye before his death by king Henry the Sixt, unto whom she bare two sonnes and a daughter; after whose death she was privately re-married unto king Edward the Fourth, the first day of May, at his manner of Grafton in Northampton shire, an. 1464, and in the next yeere following, upon the six-and-twentieth of May, was crowned queene at Westminster, with all due solemnities. She was his wife eighteene yeares eleven moneths and nine days, no more for-

---

* No. 265.

tunate in attaining to the heighth of all worldly dignity, then unfortunate in murder of her sonnes, and loſſe of her own libertye; for in the beginning of king Edward's raigne, ſhe was forced to take ſanctuary at Weſtminſter wherin her firſt ſonne, prince Edwarde, was borne; and at his death did the like in feare of the protectour: and laſtly, having all her lands and poſ-ſeſſions ſiezed upon by king Henry the Seventh, lived in meane eſtate in the monaſtery of Bermonſey in Southwarke, where not long after ſhee left the troubles of her life, and injoyed a quiet portion or burying-place by her laſt huſband, king Edward, at Windſore."

The king, queen, and figure with the cap, are habited in blue lined with ermine; the crowns, ſceptres, &c. are gold. The prince is in red, as is the figure next the king. The earl's coat as it is blazoned; his legs are blue. Caxton is in black. The figures behind are in pink. The throne, arras, and carpet, are red and gold; the floor is green, the walls of a lead colour, and the ceiling blue with gold ſpots. The book is pink, with gilt leaves.

ANTIQUITIES OF ENGLAND.

No. XLVIII.

RICHARD THE THIRD, &c.

CONTAINS a portrait of prince Edward (only fon to king Henry the Sixth) who was murdered at Tewkefbury. Another of lady Ann, daughter and coheir of Richard Nevil, earl of Warwick and Salifbury, who was firft married to the above prince Edward, and afterwards re-married to Richard duke of Glocefter. Another of Richard duke of Glocefter (afterwards king Richard the Third) eighth and youngeft fon of Richard duke of York, and Cecily Nevil his wife. And another of Edward Plantagenet, prince of Wales, the only fon of the above Richard and Ann: he died very young, in the life-time of his father.—The originals of thefe portraits are drawn by the hand of John Rous, the celebrated hiftorian of Warwickfhire *.

An authentic portrait of king Richard the Third can hardly be found: the prefent one we may, I believe, in great meafure depend upon, becaufe it was drawn by a man who was living at the time in which he reigned. In the chronicles and hiftories of this kingdom Richard is ufually defcribed as a man of little ftature, and greatly deformed; but one of the moft learned and elegant authors of the prefent day has taken great pains to prove, that he was neither deformed in perfon, nor fo wicked in his actions as has been generally reprefented.—The portrait here given of Edward, the fon of king Richard, is the only one of him extant that I know of. He was born in the caftle of Middleham (fays Speed) near Richmond, in the county of York, A. D. 1473, and being under four years of age, was created earl of Salifbury by his uncle, king Edward the Fourth, in the

---

* The MS. from which this plate is copied, is preferved in the Cottonian Library, and it is marked Julius F. IV. The figures from part of a genealogical table of the family of Beauchamp, earl of Warwick, the whole of whofe life is reprefented in a multitude of delineations copied in the fecond volume of the Donba Angelcynnan, or, THE MANNERS AND CUSTOMS, &c. OF THE ENGLISH.—Thefe figures are drawn with a pen, and are all of one colour (namely, brown), apparently bifter.

feventeenth

feventeenth year of his reign. But his father Richard, in the firſt year of his uſurpation, created him prince of Wales, the 24th of Auguſt, A. D. 1483, he being then ten years of age; and the crown was entailed unto him by the parliament; but he died before his father, about the ſame time that his mother deceaſed.

XLIX

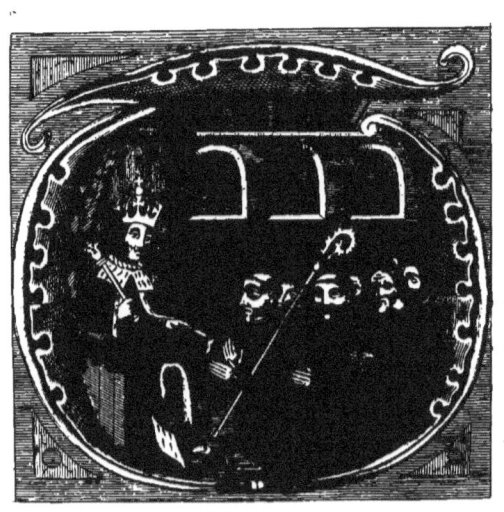

ANTIQUITIES OF ENGLAND.

THE two following plates are taken from a MS. preferved in the Harleian library, which is fairly written on vellum, and moft elegantly bound in crimfon velvet, edged with crimfon and gold thread, with taffels of the fame at each corner, and lined on the infide with crimfon damafk: on the cover are five boffes of filver, wrought and gilt, the middle one of which contains the arms of Henry the Seventh, and the other four the portcullis, gilt, on a field party per pale, argent and vert, in enamel. It is made faft with two clafps, on each of which is a red rofe of Lancafter, and half an angel proceeding out of a cloud on the top.

The book itfelf contains four original indentures, made between the king (Henry VII.) and John Iflip, abbot of Weftminfter, fpecifying the number of maffes, collects, &c. which were to be faid for the departed fouls of the king's father, wife, and other relations, &c. and provifion to be made for thirteen poor men by the king, with many other like matters. —See the catalogue of the Harleian MSS. No. 1498.

No. XLIX.
KING HENRY THE SEVENTH.

Is the king (Henry VII.) giving the book to John Iflip, the abbot of Weftminfter, who kneels before him, bearing his crozier on his left arm (Weftminfter being a mitred abbey). Behind him are divers of his monks, and fome of the almfmen or beadfmen (mentioned above) with their beads in their hands.

The perfon and character of this king are drawn as follows, by Grafton:

" He was a man of bodie but leane and fpare, albeit mightie and ftrong therewith; of perfonage and ftature, fomewhat higher then the meane fort of men be, of a wonderfull beautye and fayre complexion; of countinance mery and fmiling, efpeciallye in his communication; his eyes gray, his teeth fingle, and heare thinne; of witt in all thinges quicke and prompt; of a princely ftomacke, and haute courage. In great perilles, doubtfull affayres, and matters of waightie importance, fupernaturell, and in maner devine; for fuch thinges as he went about, he did them advifedly, and not without great deliberation and breathing, to the intent that, amongft all men,

men, his wit and prudence might be noted and regarded; for he was not ignorant that acts and doings were especially noted and marked with the eies of many a person; and therefore a prince ought as farr to excell and surmount all meane personages in wisedome and pollicie, as he precelleth other in estate and dignitie : For what man will give credite or regarde to him whom he hath proved to be light, wilde, and lascivous of condicions? Besides this, he was sober, moderate, honest, affable, curteous, bounteous, so much abhorred pride and arrogancie, that he was ever sharpe and quicke to them which were noted or spotted with that crime; and there was no man with him, being never so much in his favour, or having never so much auchthoritie, that either durst or could do any thing as his awne phantasy did serve him, without the consent and agrement of other.—What shall I say more? Although his mother were never so wise (as she was both wittie and wise) yet her will was brydeled, and her doynges restrayned. And this regiment he saide he kept to the intent that he might be called a king, whose office is to rule, and not to be ruled of other.

" He was also an indifferent and sure justicier, by the which one thing he allured to him the heartes of many people, becaufe they lived quetly and in rest, out of all opresion and molestation of the nobilitie and riche personnes. And to this severity of his, was joyned and annexed a certain merciful pittie, whiche he did often showe to such as had offended, and by his lawes were hindred and merced; for such of his subjectes as were fyned or amerced by his justices, to their great impoverishing, he at one time or another did helpe relieve, and set forward : wherby it appeared that he would have the same penalties for other offences and crimes revived and stirred up agayne, whiche was a playne argument that he did ufe his rigour only (as he said himselfe) to bring lowe, and abate the high stomachs of the wild people, nourished in seditious and civil rebellions, and not for the greedy desire of richesse, or hunger of money—although such as were afflicted would cry out and say, that it was done more for the desire of gain than for any prudent pollicie or politick provision."

The king's robe is red, and lined with ermine; his hose are a flesh colour: the crown and scepter are gold. All the figures behind are in black : the almsmen wear golden badges on their left shoulders. The elbow of the throne is green; the canopy and curtains crimson; the arras a deep red, and the wall and pavement are of stone colour: the cieling is blue, powdered with golden stars : the letter is blue, white, and red, on a gold ground.

No. L.

CONFIRMATION OF THE DEEDS OF ALMS.

REPRESENTS a monk ſtanding before a deſk, and reading the abſtract of the firſt deed (according to the directions therein contained), a judge, with other miniſters of the law, aſſiſting on the right hand, and abbot Iſlip with his monks on the left.

Beſides the donations contained in theſe indentures, king Henry built a ſumptuous chapel at Weſtminſter.

" In the year of our Lord 1503 (ſays Stow) took down the chapel of our Lady, above the eaſt end of the high altar at Weſtminſter, as well as a tavern near adjoining, called the White Roſe, and in the ſame place, or plot of ground, on the 24 day of January, the firſt ſtone of our Ladies chapel was laid, by the hands of John Iſlip, abbat of Weſtminſter; Sir Reginald de Bray, knight of the Garter; Doctor Barons, maſter of the Rolls; and Dr. Wall, chaplaine to the king; maſter Hugh Oldham, chaplaine to the counteſs of Derby and Richmond, the king's mother; Sir Edward Stanhope, knight, and divers others: upon which ſtone was engraven the day, the year, &c.—The charges in building this chapel (as I have been informed) amounted to the ſummes of 14,000 pounds.— This chappel Leland calls the miracle of the world; for any man that ſees it may well ſay, that " all elegancy of worſhip and matter is couched in it:" and this building the king directed chiefly " to be a place of ſepulture for himſelf and all his poſterity; where in at this time is to be ſeene his owne tombe, moſt gorgeous and great, made all of ſolid braſs."

Thus far mine author. And in another place in his Survey, he remarks that " the alter and ſepulchre of the ſame king (Henry the Seventh) wherein his body reſteth in this his new chappel, was made and finiſhed in the yeere 1519, by one Peter, a painter of Florence, for which he received 1000 ſterling for the ſtuff and workmanſhip, at the hands of the king's executors, Richard biſhop of Wincheſter; Richard biſhop of London; Thomas biſhop of Durham; John biſhop of Rocheſter; Thomas duke of Norfolk,

ANTIQUITIES OF ENGLAND.

Norfolk, treafurer of England; Charles earl of Worcefter, the king's chamberlaine; John Fineaux, knight, chief juftice of the King's Bench; Robert Reade, knight, chief juftice of the Common Pleas."

The abbot and his monks are in black; the judge is in red, lined with white; the figure next him is in red, the next in blue, and the next in red; the feat and ftep are green; the defk the book lies on is crimfon; the wall and pavement are of a ftone colour; the letter as before, red, white, and blue, on a gilt ground.

This plate is copied from the fame MS. as the foregoing.—See page 97.

LI

ADDITIONS TO THE WORK.

WE have thus far brought down the series of kings, &c. from the reign of Edward the Confessor, which have been diligently collected, as well as the greatest care and attention bestowed to make them as complete as possible: yet, since the beginning and continuation of this work, several curious matters, which unavoidably had escaped notice, have occurred, and are here given in chronological order.

No. LI*.

HENRY THE FIRST.

REPRESENTS king Henry the First bewailing the fatal and unfortunate end of his children, who are represented below struggling in vain with the tempest, wherein they perished. This circumstance is related as follows, by Speed:

"Prince William, who now wanted but only the name of a king, commanded another shippe to be prepared for himselfe, his brethren and sisters, with many other nobles and gallant courtiers both of England and Normandy, who plying the mariners with pots and wine (therin being instruments of their owne calamity approaching) made them bragge to out-saile the king's shippe before; and in the night putting forth from land, with a merry gale, made way over the dancing waves as swift as an arrow: but (as if the heavens would have king Henries too great felicities allaid, and tempered with sense of courtly variety) in the midst of their jollity and singing (alas! they sang their last, and little thought on death!) for suddainely the shippe dashed against a rocke, not very far from the shoare, at which fearfull disaster a hideous cry arose, all of them shifting (and yet through amazednels not knowing how to shift) to save themselves from the

---

* This plate is copied from Claudius, D. 2.

danger:

danger: for God repaying the reward for finne, fuffer'd not thofe unnatural wantons (for fuch were many of them, faith Paris) to have chriftian buriall, and fo fwallowed them up in the fea, when her waves were moft calme. Prince William gat fpeedily into the cocke-boate, and might well have efcaped, had not hee pittied his fifter, the counteffe of Perche, crying unto him for helpe, when turning the boat to her ayde, fo many ftrived to get in (every man in fuch a cafe efteeming his life as much as a prince) that with their weight it prefently funcke, and of fo princely a traine no one efcaped to relate that dolefull tragedie, fave only a bafe fellow (a butcher fome fay) who fwamme all night upon the maine-mafte, and got fhoare in the morning, with much danger of life.

" This was the moft unfortunate fhipwrack that ever hapned in our feas, bringing an inconceivable heavineffe to the king and whole ftate: for therin perifhed prince William duke of Normandy, the joy of his father, and hope of his nation; Richard, his bafe brother; his fifter Maud, counteffe of Perche; Richard earle of Chefter, with his wife lady Lucy, the king's niece by his fifter; Adela Otwell, the earle's brother; the young duke's governor; divers of the king's chiefe officers, and moft of the princes; Geffrey Riddle, Robert Manduit, William Bigod, Geffrey arch-deacon of Hereford, Walter de Crucie, and many other of prime note and efteeme, to the number of one hundred and fixty perfons, none of their bodies being found, though great fearch was made for them."

The king is habited in deep blue; his robe is light pink lined with red; the feat is of a ftone colour; the back ground on the right fide is red and filver, and on the left blue and gold; the frame red and blue; the two children blue, and the two attendants blue and red; the fhip a light brown, and the water green.

No. LII.

No. LII*.

KING JOHN.

Is king John, who is reprefented hunting. This illumination is at the head of a foreft charter.

Speed, after repeating the fcandals which the monks unjuftly threw upon king John in their writings, makes note of his actions as follows :

" His works of devotion were inferior to none, as his foundations declare at Beauly, Farrington, Malmefbury, and Dublin, and that other for nunnes at Godftow, by Oxford, from which fome have interpreted that prophefie of Merlin as meant of him :

> Sith virgins-gifts to maids he gave
> 'Mongft bleffed faints God will him fave.

" His acts and orders for weale-publike were beyond moft, he being either firft, or the chiefeft, who appointed thofe noble formes of civill government in London, and moft cities and incorporate townes of England, endowing them alfo with the greateft franchifes ; the firft who caufed fterling money to be here coyned : the firft who ordained the honourable ceremonies in creation of earles : the firft who fetled the rates and meafures for wine, bread, cloth, and fuch-like neceffaries of commerce : the firft who planted englifh lawes and officers in Ireland, and both annexed that kingdome and faftned Wales to the crowne of England, thereby making amends for his loffes in France ; and thence, amongft all the Englifh monarchs, he was the firft who enlarged the royal ftile with Lorde of Ireland : a matter of greater import for England's peace, than all the French titles ever yet have proved. Whofe whole courfe of life and actions wee cannot fhut with any truer euloge, than that which an ancient author hath conferr'd on him : " Princeps quidem magnus erat, fed minus fælix ; atque ut Marius, utramque fortunam expertus."—Doubtleffe he was a prince more

---

* This plate is from Claudius, D. 2.

great

REGAL AND ECCLESIASTICAL

great than happy, and one who, like Marius, had tried both fides of Fortune's wheele."

The king is dreffed in a light red tunic, and a blue robe; the horfe is grey, and the trappings red; the ftag and the rabbits are of a dun colour; the dogs proper; trees and ground green; the back ground is blue and red, with gold fquares.

No. LIII.

LIII

ANTIQUITIES OF ENGLAND.

No. LIII*.

EDWARD THE THIRD, AND DAVID KING OF SCOTLAND.

Is Edward the Third, and David king of Scotland, who are reprefented hand in hand; an emblem of the peace confirmed between them. This illumination is at the head of the articles of the peace, which are moft elegantly written, and the initial letter of each article embellifhed with the royal arms of England, quartered with thofe of France. This peace was concluded in the year 1357, at the conftant fupplication and intreaties of Joan, wife to David, (who was fifter to Edward) after he had been kept clofe prifoner for the fpace of eleven years in the caftle of Odiam. Hollingfhead relates the matter fully as follows:

" David king of Scotland, fhortly after the truce was concluded betwixte Englande and Fraunce, was fette at libertye, paying for his ranfom the fumme of one hundrethe thoufand markes, as Jourdon fayeth; but whether hee meaneth Scottifhe or fterling money, I cannot faye: he alfo was bounde by covenant, nowe upon his deliverance, to caufe the caftelles in Nidefdale to be rafed, which were knowen to be evill neighbours to the Englifhe borderers, as Dunfrife, Dalfwinton, Morton, Dunfdere, and other nine. His wife, queene Joan, made fuche earnefte fute to hir brother, king Edwarde, for hir hufbandes diliverance, that king Edwarde was contented to releafe him upon the payment of fo fmall a portion of money, and performaunce of the covenauntes for the rafing of thofe caftells; although Froiffart fayth that hee was covenaunted to pay for his deliveraunce, within the terme of ten years, five hundrethe thoufande nobles, and for furety of that payment to fende into Englande fufficient hoftages, as the earles of Douglafs, Murrey, Mar, Sutherlande, and Fiffe, the baron of Vefcye, and Sir William Camoife. Alfo he covenaunted never to wear armour agaynft king Edwarde, within his realme of Englande, nor confent that his fubjects fhould doe; and further fhoulde, upon his returne home, doe the befte he coulde to caufe the Scottes to agree that their countrie fhould holde of him

* From Nero, D. VI. as is alfo the following plate.

106   REGAL AND ECCLESIASTICAL

in fee, and that he and his fucceffoures, kings of Scotland, fhould doe homage to the king of Englande, and his fucceffors, for the realme of Scotland."

Edward is dreffed in light pink lined with ermine, and blue fleeves. The king of Scotland is in red, and his collar is gold. The back ground is blue and gold; and the letter blue, on a gilt ground. The arms are proper.

No. LIV.

LIV

No. LIV.

JOHN, KING OF FRANCE.

Is a portrait of John, king of France, who was brought prisoner into England by Edward the Black Prince.

" Now approached the time (fays Grafton) that the prince of Wales had made provifion of fhips, and furniture to the fame, for the conveyaunce and bringing of the French king, and his other prifoners, into England. And when he had all things in readineffe, he called unto him the lord Dalbert, the lorde Mufident, the lord Lafpare, the lorde of Punyers, and the lorde of Rofen, and gave them commaundemaunt to keepe the countrie there untill his returne againe.

" Then he tooke the fea, and certaine lordes of Gafcoyne with him. The Frenche kinge was in a veffell by himfelfe, to be the more at his eafe, and was accompanied with two hundreth men of armes, and two thoufand archers. For it was fhewed the prince that the three eftates, by whome the realme of Fraunce was governed, had layd in Normandye and Crotoye two great armyes, to the entent to meete with him, and to get the Frenche king out of his handes, if they might. But their appered no fuch matter; and yet they were on the fea xi dayes, and on the xii daye they arrived at Sandwich. Then they iffued out of their fhip, and landed, and lay there all that night, and taryed there two dayes after to refrefhe them; and on the third day they roade to Cauntorburie.

" When the king of England knew of their coming, he commaunded the citizens of London to prepare themfelves and their citie, and to make the fame feemely and meete to receyve fuche a man as the French king was; whiche the citezens of London did accordingly.

" And from Cauntorbury they came to Rochefter, and there taryed a daye, and from thence the next daye to London, where they were honourably receyved; and fo they were in every good towne they paffed.

" The French king roade through London on a white courfer well apparelled, and the prince on a little black hobby by him. This was (fays Hollingfhead) the foure and twentieth day of May; and they were with greate honour joyfully received of the citizens into the citie of London,

and

and fo conveyed to the pallace of Weftminfter, where the king fitting in Weftminfter Hall receyved the Frenche king, and after conveyed hym to a lodging for him appoynted, where he laye a feafon; but after hee was removed to the Savoy, whiche was at that time a goodly houfe, apperteyning to the duke of Lancafter, though afterwards it was brent and deftroyed by Wat Tyler, and Jacke Strawe, and their companie."

The king is in blue lined with ermine, pink fleeves and hofe, and a gold collar. The back ground is gold, and the ornamented frame is blue.

This is from the fame MS. as the former.

LV

ANTIQUITIES OF ENGLAND.

No. LV*.

GEOFRY DE LUCY, AND MARY DE ST. PAUL.

THE figure at the top is Geofry de Lucy, fuppofed to be the fon of that Geofry de Lucy mentioned in the reign of Edward the Firſt, and one of the knights that attended Edward the Third into France.

The figure of a lady, at the bottom of the plate, is Mary de St. Paul, (counteſs of Pembroke) who was the daughter of Guy de Chaſtilian, earl of St. Paul. She was married to Aymer de Valence, earl of Pembroke, who was murdered in France in 1323; after which (according to Stow) ſhe was re-married to Laundas, who was taken with the priſoners in the attempt to ſurprize the caſtle of Calais, in the time of Edward the Third.—This curious adventure is thus briefly related by Baker:

"In the year 1349, the 23 of Edward the Third, Geoffry de Charmy, captain of St. Omer, agreed with Aymry of Pavia, whom king Edward had left governour of Callice, to render it up for twenty thouſand crownes; whiche king Edward hearing of, ſent to Aymery, and charged him with this perfidiouſneſs; whereupon Aymery comes to the king, and humbly defiring pardon, promiſeth to handle the matter ſo as ſhall be to the king's advantage, and therupon is ſente back to Callice. The king, the night before the time of agreement, arrives with three hundred men at armes, and ſix hundred archers. Monſieur de Charmy ſets out likewiſe the ſame night from St. Omer's with his forces, and ſent a hundred men before with the crownes to Aymery. The men are let in at a poſtern gate, the crowns received, and aſſured to be all weight: which done the gates of the town are opened, and out marches the king before day to encounter Monſieur de Charmy, who perceiving himſelfe betrayed, defended himſelfe the beſt he could, and put king Edward to hard bickering, who for that he would not be known there in perſon, put himſelf and the prince under the colours of the lord Walter Manny, and was twice beaten down on his knees by Monſieur de Riboumont, a hardy knight, (with whom he fought hand to hand) and yet recovered, and in the end took Riboumont priſoner. Charmy

* This plate, with No. 57, 59, and 60, are all from Nero, D. VII.

was likewife taken, and all his forces defeated. King Edward the night after (which was the firft of the new year) feafted with prifoners, and gave Riboumont, in honour of his valour, a rich chaplet of pearl which himfelf wore on his head (for a new-year's gift) forgave him his ranfome, and fet him at liberty.—Amongft the prifoners who were taken on this occafion, were Geffrey Charney, and his fon, Edward de Renty, Robert Danquil, Otto de Gulo, the baron Mactingham, Baldina Saylly, Henry de Piees, Garinus Baylofe, Peter Renell, Peter Dargemole, Eftace de Riplemount, and many other, lords, knights, and baronets, who were chafed and ranne away with their auncients, as the lord de Mounmarice, alfo Laundas, who maryed the ladie Saint Paul, countefs of Pembroke, in England; alfo the lord Fenas, the L. Planckes, and another Euftace de Riplemount. There were flaine in the fkirmifh, the lord Henry de Boys, the lord Archibald, and many others, whofe names the conquerors were not able to certify."

This Mary de St. Paul was a devout and religious lady, poffeffed of a confiderable dowry, which fhe beftowed in pious and charitable ufes. She here holds an image of gold of the Virgin Mary, which fhe gave to the Abbey of St. Alban's. She alfo founded Pembroke Hall, Cambridge, in the year 1343, and died 1377.

The top figure is in blue, with a pink hood and black cap; back ground is blue and gold, and the frame is blue. The lady's habit is cloth of gold, fo is her head drefs; and the image is gold: the altar is marble, and the back ground a deep red; the whole enclofed in a blue frame.

No. LVI.

JOHN GOWER.

REPRESENTS the portrait of John Gower, a famous Englifh poet, who was cotemporary with Chaucer, and greatly affifting with him in refining the Englifh language. He was author of the Confeffio Amantis, in Englifh; the Speculum Meditantis, in French; and the Vox Clamantis, in Latin; from a MS*. of which laft work the prefent portrait is taken; it is preferved in the Cotton Library. He is here reprefented fhooting at the world, with thefe lines over the picture:

Ab mundum mitto mea jacula bunque fagitto;
At ubi juftus erit nulla fagitta ferit,
Sed male biventes hos bulnero tranfgredientes,
Confcius ergo fibi fe fperuletur ibi.

In Englifh fomething like this:
My darts and arrows to the world I fend;
Amongft the juft my arrows fhall not fall,
But evil doers through and through I wound;
Who confcious of their faults may learn to mend.

" The famous poet, John Gower (fays Stow) was a man not much unlike the other (Chaucer) in excellency of wit, learning, or poffeffions. He builded a great part of S. Mary Oueries church in Southwark, then new re-edified; on the north fide of the which church he prepared for his bones a refting place, where fomewhat after the old fafhion he lyeth right fumptuoufly buried in a tombe of ftone, with his image alfo of ftone lying over him, the haire of his heade awburne long to his fhoulders, and curling up, a fmall forked beard, and on his head a garland or chaplet of rofes red, 4 in number, an habit of purple damafked downe to his feet, a coller of effes of gold about hys necke, under his head the likenefs of the 3 bookes which he compiled. His tombe arched was beautified with his armes, and

---

* This is in the Cotton Library, marked Tib. A. iv. and the whole is of one colour, namely, dark brown.

the likenefs of angels with pofies in Latine. Befide, in the wall were painted three virgins crowned, one of the which was written Charity, and held this device, " En toy qui filz de Dieu le pere fauue foit, qui gift fubs cefte perre." The fecond Mercie, with this device, " O bon Jefu ! fait ta mercie alme dont le corps gift jcy." The third Pittie, with this device, " Pour ta pite Jefu regard, et mete cefte alme in fauue garde." All which is now wafhed out, and the image defaced by cutting off the nofe and ftriking off his hands.—He died An. Dom. 1402, about 80 years of age."

No. LVII.

L. Talbot, and had iſſue by him a daughter, who dyed young: Philip and Iſabell, both dying iſſueleſs."

The figure is in deep crimſon, lined with white, the coronet round his head is gold; the ſwan is ſilver; the back ground blue and gold, and the frame red.

LVIII

No. LVIII*.

DUEL BEFORE THE KING.

ANCIENTLY, when any matter of importance was brought before the juftices, which could not be proved by witnefs, combat was granted; and in this cafe, if the accufed was vanquifhed, he was convicted of the crime he was accufed of; and if the accufer, he was punifhed as a perjured man and a falfe witnefs. The culprit was then executed (if he was not flain in the combat) without any further examination.—This was the cafe between two efquires in the reign of Richard the Second. The one of Navarre accufed an Englifh efquire, called John Welch, of treafon; for trial thereof a day was appointed for a combat, which was to be performed in the king's palace at Weftminfter. Accordingly being met, there was a valiant fight betwixt them; but at laft the Englifhman was the conqueror, and the vanquifhed Frenchman was defpoiled of his armour, drawn to Tyburn, and there hanged for his untruth.

The order of the combat, with the procefs, was as follows:—The accufed ftrongly denying the fact alledged againft him, threw down his gauntlet, or any other gage, calling the accufer a lyar, and thereby challenging him to combat; then the other took up the gage of the accufed, and threw down his own, declaring his willingnefs to prove by battle the truth of his affertions: the gages were then fealed, and delivered to the marfhal, and leave to combat demanded of the king; which if he granted, a day and place was then appointed, by which time a fcaffold was erected for the king and his attendants (the earl marfhal, and high conftable of England) who were to fee that no undue advantage might be taken by either party; and the lifts were railed round.—This method of trial was not often put in execution.

The above illumination was made about the reign of Richard the Second, whofe portrait the figure of the king much refembles. In this king's reign, Henry earl of Derby challenged Thomas Moubray, duke of Norfolk, to fingle combat.

* This is from Nero, D. 17.

REGAL AND ECCLESIASTICAL

The armour of the two fighting figures is filver; the plates at their elbows, and their girdles, are gilt. The firft figure to the right is the fame. The king is in light pink, with a blue robe lined with ermine. The figure next the king is in filver armour, the body of which is purple. The back ground is red, flowered; the ground of the lifts is green, and the rails are red. The letter is blue and red, on a purple ground, with a gilt edge.

LIX

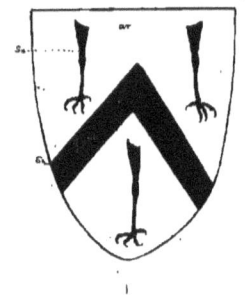

No. LIX*.

ROBERT CHAMBERLEYN.

THE fingular figure here reprefented, is, in the original, faid to be the portrait of a knight named Robert Chamberleyn, who is fuppofed to have been in France with Henry the Fifth, at the battle of Agincourt. This curious painting, which is placed amongft the benefactors to the Abbey of St. Alban's (in the great book mentioned before) has a date put by the fide of it, which follows the name of the knight, viz. 1417; the time moft likely that the donation was made from him to the abbey, and probably left them by his laft will; which is the reafon why he is reprefented upon his knees, in a praying pofture, offering up a fcrole, which is received by a hand above, fignifying that his prayer was heard by Almighty God. On the fcrole is written, in the character of that time,.

" Miferere mei Deus !"

" Have mercy upon me, O God !"

The chief reafon for engraving this picture (as no account can be given of the family or hiftory of the perfon reprefented, unlefs his arms underneath may lead to any difcovery) was for the reprefentation of the armour worn by the knights at that time, which is here fo exactly delineated, and fo much more perfect than in general it can be found.—A modern may furvey, with wonder, the great weight of iron under which thofe hardy warriors fought, and to whofe prowefs England owes fo much, and who fo far advanced her glory in the fingular victories obtained againft our rival foes.

The body of this knight's armour is filver, done over with a light vernifh, and flowered; the armour on his arms, legs and thighs, as well as his

* This is from the fame MS. as No. LVII.

gauntlet

118   REGAL AND ECCLESIASTICAL

gauntlet and helmet, are filvered over, without any vernifh, only flightly fhaded; the ground he kneels upon is green, and the back ground is blue, diamonded with ftronger and lighter colours; the border is gilt. The field of the arms below, is argent; the legs, &c. fable.

No. LX.

LX

No. LX.

THOMAS RAMRYGE, ABBOT OF ST. ALBAN'S.

THIS is a very curious plate, and reprefents Thomas Ramryge, who was abbot of St. Alban's at the time in which the curious catalogue of the benefactors to that abbey was compleated (about the year 1484).—This book, called the Golden Regifter, we have had frequent occafion to mention, and feveral valuable portraits are engraved from it, as has been feen in the courfe of the work.

Ramryge is reprefented upon his knees, praying to the Holy Trinity, pictured as a fort of altar piece, and on the altar before is refted his mitre (St. Alban's being a mitred abbey).—By the fide of the abbot is a fcrole, on which is written,

"Sancta Trinitas, unus Deus, miferis animis T. Ramryge."
"Holy Trinity, one God, have mercy upon the foul of T. Ramryge."

Which is entirely agreeable to the zeal of the times.—Part of his epitaph is preferved by Weever, which runs thus:

"Hic jacet - - - Thomas, Abbas huius Monafterii."

"This is the laft abbot (adds that author) for whom I find any infcription or epitaph, and the laft in my catalogue; whofe furname was Ramrige."

"Vir fuis temporibus tam dilectus Deo quam hominibus, propter que caufas varias nomen in perpetua benedictione apud pofteros habens."—(He was an excellent man in his time, beloved as well by God as men; for which reafon his name was had in perpetual bleffings amongft pofterity.)— Saith this fame Golden Regifter, in a fubfequent entry.

The abbot is in black; the altar is blue, and the pavement dark and light green; the mitre white, bordered with gold. The figure of God is in red, and a blue robe: the glory is gold, on a yellow ground; the crofs is green, and the figure of Chrift flefh colour. The back ground is red and gold: the letter is blue, white and red.

F I N I S.

AN INDEX FOR FINDING THE MANUSCRIPTS, &c.

MENTIONED IN THIS BOOK.

Cotton Library, British Museum.
PLATE.
I. - - - - Vespasianus, A. VIII.
II. III. IV. V. VI. ⎫
VII. X. XI. XII. ⎬ Vitellius, A. XIII.
XIII. - - - ⎭
VIII. LI. LII. - Claudius, D. II.
IX. - - - - Julius, A. XI.
XIV. XV. XVI. ⎫
LIII. LIV. - ⎬ Nero, D. VI.
XXXIV. XXXV. ⎫
XXXVI. XLIV. ⎬
LV. LVII. LIX. ⎬ Nero, D. VII.
LX. - - - ⎭
XLVIII. - - Julius, E. IV.
LVI. - - - Tiberius, A. IV.
LVIII. - - - Nero, D. XVII.

Harleian Library, British Museum.
PLATE.
XX. XXI. XXII. ⎫
XXIII. XXIV. ⎬
XXV. XXVI. ⎬ No. 1319.
XXVII. XXVIII. ⎬
XXIX. XXX. ⎬
XXXI. XXXIII. ⎭
XXXVII. - - - No. 4866.
XLI. - - - No. 2278.
XLV. - - - No. 4826.
XLIX. L. - - No. 1498.

Royal Library, British Museum.
PLATE.
XIX. - - - - 20. B. 6.
XXXII. XXXVIII. 18. E. 2.
XLIII. - - - 15. E. 6.
XLVI. - - - 15. E. 4.

Westminster Abbey.
PLATE.
XVII. XVIII.

Bodleian Library, Oxford.
PLATE.
XXXIX. XLII. - Digby. 233.

Bennet College Library, Cambridge.
PLATE.
XL.

Archbishop's Library, Lambeth.
PLATE.
XLVII. - - No. 265.

This INDEX, and the following, were drawn up by JOHN FENN, Esq; F. A. S. of East Derham, in Norfolk, who was so kind as to permit the author to print them from his MS. He therefore takes this opportunity to return his sincere acknowledgments to that gentleman, not only for these, but several other special favours received from him.

A CATALOGUE OF THE PLATES

IN THE

REGAL AND ECCLESIASTICAL ANTIQUITIES OF ENGLAND.

Plate No.	Kings, Princes, Noblemen, Bishops, Knights, Authors, &c.	when born	began to reign	died, or murdered	MS. when written, or Illuminations drawn.
I.	King Edgar adoring our Saviour	943	959	973	966
II.	Edward the confessor	1002	1041	1066	
	Egitha his queen, daughter of } at a banquet 1053.			1074	
	Goodwin earl of Kent			1053	
III	Harold II. shot into the eye } bat. of Haftings			1066	1066	Edw. I. 1272—1307
	William the Conqueror } - 1066 -			1066	1088	
IV	William Rufus, in his robes of ftate	1056	1088	1100	
V.	Henry I. furnamed Beauclerk, in robes of ftate	1070	1100	1135	
LI.	Henry I. bewailing the lofs of his children, 1120.				
XXXIV.	Maud, queen of Henry I. 1101.				1377—1461
VI.	Stephen, in the drefs of the time	1104	1135	1154	1272—1307
VII.	Henry II. in his coronation robes	1133	1154	1189	
VIII.	Henry II. difputing with Thomas of Becket, abp of Canterbury, 1162			1171	
IX.	Thomas of Becket murdered at the altar			1171	1172
X	Richard I. imprifoned, 1192—wounded, 1199	1157	1189	1199	1272—1307
LII.	King John on horfeback, hunting a ftag	1160	1199	1216	
XI	King John in robes of ftate, receiving a cup			1216	
XII.	Henry III. crowned by	1206	1216	1272	
	Peter de la Roche, bp of Winchefter, 1204			1238	Edw. I. 1272—1307
	Henry Blont, abbot of Glocefter, 1205			1224	
XIII.	Edward I. on his throne, receiving the } pope's bull from	1239	1272	1307	
	Abp of Canterbury, and others.				
XIV.	Edward II giving his marfhal's commiffion to	1284	1307	1327	
	Thomas of Brotherton, earl of Norfolk, } 1315	1300		1338	
LIII.	Edward III. confirming the peace with				
	David II. king of Scotland, 1357	1321	1329	1370	14th Century.
I IV.	John the Good, king of France, prifoner, 1357	1319	1350	1364	
XV.	Edward III. giving the conquered provinces } of France to	1312	1327	1377	
	Edward the Black Prince, 1362	1330		1376	
XXXV.	Joan of Kent, wife of Edw. the Black Prince			1386	
LV.	Geofrey de Lucy, and				1377—1461
	Mary de St. Paul, countefs of Pembroke			1377	

R

CATALOGUE OF THE PLATES.

Plate No.	Kings, Princes, Noblemen, Bishops, Knights, Authors, &c.	when born.	began to reign.	died, or murdered.	Date of MSS.
XVI.	John of Gaunt, duke of Lancafter, as high fteward, and - - - - -	1340		1399	14th Century
	Thomas of Woodftock, high conftable, 1377	1355		1397	
XXXVI.	Conftance, wife of John of Gaunt, and daughter of the king of Caftile -	1354		1394	Richard II. 1377.
	Margaret, duchefs of Norfolk, daughter of Thomas of Brotherton - -			1399	Edward IV. 1461.
LVII.	Thomas of Woodftock, duke of Glocefter	1355		1397	
XXXVII.	Geofrey Chaucer - - - - - - -	1328		1400	15th Century
LVI.	John Gower, a poet, fhooting at the world	1323		1402	
XVII.	Richard II. crowned by - - - - -	1366	1377	1400	
	Simon Sudbury, abp of Canterbury, 1375, and			1381	
	Nicholas de Lytlington, abbot of Weft-minfter, 1361 - - - - -			1386	Richard II. 1377—1387
	Henry earl of Derby (afterwards Hen.4.) with the fword - - - -	1366			
XVIII.	Ann of Bohemia, queen of Richard II. - crowned by		1382	1394	
	W. Courtney, abp. of Canterbury, 1381			1396	
XIX.	Richard II. on his throne, attended by officers of his court, and receiving a book from a Celeftine monk - - -				1377—1399
LVIII.	Richard II. prefent at a combat, attended by earl marfhal and high conftable of England				1377—1399
XX.	Francis de la Marque, a French gentleman, & Janico D'Artois, a Gafcoigne knt. 1399.				
XXI.	Richard II. in Ireland, knights (1399)				
	Henry, fon of the duke of Lancafter (afterwards Henry V.) - -	1388			
XXII.	Tho. Spencer, earl of Glocefter, confers with Mac Murrough, the Irifh rebel.			1401	
XXIII.	Tho. Arundel, abp. of Canterbury, reading the pope's bull - - - - - -			1413	Hen. IV. 1401—1413
XXIV.	Richard II. at Conway caftle, confulting with				
	John Montacute, earl of Salifbury - -			1401	
	Thomas Merks, bifhop of Carlifle, 1397			1401	
	John Holland, duke of Exeter (earl of Huntingdon) and - - -			1401	
	Thomas Holland, duke of Surrey - -			1401	
XXV.	Dukes of Exeter & Surrey riding to Chefter				
XXVI.	The dukes of Exeter & Surrey introduced to Henry of Bolingbroke, duke of Lancafter	1367			

CATALOGUE OF THE PLATES.

Plate No.	Kings, Princes, Noblemen, Bishops, Knights, Authors, &c.	when born.	begar to reign.	died, or murdered.	Date of MSS.
XXVII.	Henry Percy, 1st earl of Northumberland persuading Richard II. to go with him to the duke of Lancaster. The earl of Salisbury, &c are with the king.			1407	
XXVIII.	The earl of Northumberland confirms by oath to Richard II. &c. the truth of his engagement.				
XXIX.	Richard II. &c. riding towards Chester, meets the earl of Northumberland with a party of soldiers.				Hen. IV. 1401—1413
XXX.	Richard II. at Flint castle, attended by the earl of Salisbury and bishop of Carlisle; respectfully saluted by Henry duke of Lancaster 20th August, 1399.				
XXXI.	Richard II. led into London by Henry duke of Lancaster; they are met by the citizens of London 1st September, 1399.				
XXXII.	Richard II. in his royal robes, resigning his crown to Henry duke of Lancaster, 29th September, 1399.				Hen. VI. 1460.
XXXIII.	Richard II.'s resignation declared in parliament, and Henry duke of Lancaster recognized for king; The bishops sit on the right, and the noblemen on the left hand of the throne; Henry earl of Northumberland, and Ralph Nevill, earl of Westmorland are standing.			1407 1425	Hen. IV. 1401—1413
XXXVIII.	Henry IV. crowned at Westminster, by Thomas Arundel, abp. of Canterbury - Richard Scrope, abp. of York, 1397 - Will. de Colchester, abbot of Westminster	1367	1399	1413 1413 1405 1421	Hen. VI. 1460.
XXXIX.	Henry IV. in his royal robes, receiving from Hoccleve a book, 1408. Nobles attending.				1408.
XL.	Henry V. on his throne, receiving from - John de Galopes a book; on the right L. de Luxemburgh, chancellor of France	1388	1413	1422 1443	Hen. V. 1413—1422
XLI.	Henry VI. surrounded by his court at Bury, & John duke of Bedford, regent of France, & Humphrey duke of Glocester, (1428-1441) receiving from Will. Curteis, abbot of Bury, a book -	1421	1422	1471 1435 1447 1440	Hen. VI. 1428—1440
XLII.	Hen. VI. on his throne, receiving a book from John Lidgate, a monk of Bury - -		1380	1440	1422—1440

CATALOGUE OF THE PLATES.

PLATE No.	KINGS, PRINCES, NOBLEMEN, BISHOPS, KNIGHTS, AUTHORS, &c.	when born.	began to reign	died, or murdered	Date of MSS.
XLIII.	Henry VI. attended by lords and ladies, and Margaret of Anjou, his queen - - receiving an account of the garter from John Talbot, earl of Shrewsbury (1442) Humphrey duke of Glocester standing by.		1445	1482 1453	Hen. VI. 1445—1453
XLIV.	Thomas Beauchamp, earl of Warwick - Margaret, his countess, daughter of Will. lord Ferrers of Groby Humphrey duke of Glocester, 4th son of Henry IV. - - - - - Eleanor, his duchess, daughter of Reginald lord Cobham.	1346		1401 1447	1377—1461
XLV.	Thomas Montacute, earl of Salisbury - receiving from John Lidgate, monk of Bury - - - a book called The Pilgrim.	1380		1428 1440	
LIX.	Sir Robert Chamberlyn, knt. 1417 - -				1417.
XLVI.	Edward IV. on his throne of state - - receiving from the author the Chronicle of England; Richard duke of Glocester - - - and other nobles standing.	1443 1453	1461	1483 1485	Edw. IV. 1461—1483
XLVII.	Edward IV. on his throne, and Elizabeth his queen, daughter of Sir Rd. Woodville, earl Rivers, and widow of Sir R. Grey. Prince Edward (afterwards Edward V.) standing. Richard duke of Glocester - - - and other nobles standing. Anth. Woodville, earl Rivers, on his knee, presenting his book, and W. Caxton, his printer, to the king, 1477	1470 1453 1411	1483	1483 1485 1483 1491	1477.
XLVIII.	Prince Edward, only son of king Henry VI. Ann, his princess, (afterwards queen of Richard III.) daughter of Richard earl of Warwick - - - - - Richard III. - - - - - - Edward prince of Wales, son of Richard the Third and Ann - - - -	1453 1453 1473	1483	1471 1485 1485 1484	1461—1509
XLIX.	Henry VII. giving a book to John Islip, abbot of Westminster, 1498 -	1455	1485	1509 1516	Hen. VII.
L.	John Islip, abbot of Westminster, hearing a deed read, attended by a judge, lawyers, and monks.			1516	1498—1509
LX.	Tho. Ramryge, abbot of St. Alban's (1484) praying to the Holy Trinity.			1526	Hen. VII. 1485—1509

SUPPLEMENT.

A

SUPPLEMENT

TO THE

REGAL and ECCLESIASTICAL

Antiquities, Manners, Customs, Arms, Habits, &c.

OF THE

ENGLISH,

By JOSEPH STRUTT.

LONDON:

Printed for the Author, and sold by Messrs. WHITE, and SON, Fleet-Street; Mr. FAULDER, New-Bond-Street; and Mr. THANE, Rupert-Street, near the Haymarket.

MDCCXCII.

SUPPLEMENT

TO THE

Horda Angelcynnan;

OR,

A compleat View of the Manners, Customs, Arms, Habits, &c.

OF THE

ENGLISH.

By JOSEPH STRUTT.

LONDON:

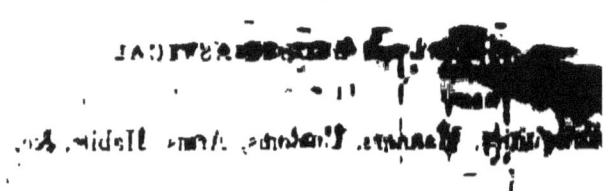

Printed for J. Nichols, and sold by Messrs. White, and Son, Fleet-street; Mr. Faulder, New Bond-street; and Mr. Trphook, Bury-street, near the Exchange.

M.DCC.LXXV.

PREFACE.

I NEED not, I presume, insist upon the usefulness of this Publication; because it is evident, that from sources so authentic as the delineations found in old manuscripts are allowed to be, we may derive much light, not only to illustrate in many instances the obscurity of Ancient History, but also to explain in a more full, and certain, manner, the obsolete customs of our ancestors. They assist us to look back upon the times of old, and we see our progenitors, as it were, in person before us; and though it must be granted, that these drawings are frequently very rude and uncouth in their appearance, it cannot be denied but that with all their defects they convey a much clearer and juster idea, of the habits and manners of the people they represent, than can be formed from the most finished, and elegant description.

The favourable reception which my two former publications of this kind met with, has encouraged me to proceed with this, which may properly be considered as a supplement to them both. In the second volume of the Manners and Customs of the English, there is a chasm, from the middle of the thirteenth century, to the end of the fourteenth; which all my diligence at that time, from the want of proper and authentic materials, was ineffectual to supply. Not long since I discovered the manuscript from which the present engravings are taken, and they are in every respect suited to remedy the deficiency I then laboured under. With this view I have laid them before the public, to whose candor and protection, I freely commit the work.

The original designs, from which the engravings, which constitute this publication, are taken, were apparently outlined with a pen, and the shadows washed in with a colour somewhat resembling bister; they are very neatly executed, and though not coeval with the facts they represent, yet they are undoubtedly faithful pictures of the customs of the age in which they were drawn.

PREFACE.

I thought it unnecessary to burthen this work with the history at length of the several delineations contained in it, and have therefore confined myself to so much of it only, as seemed absolutely requisite to explain them, without obliging the reader at all times, to have recourse to the English History, where at pleasure he may meet with fuller information.

The manuscript containing these drawings is preserved in the Royal Library at the British Museum. By the writing and dress of the figures represented therein, it is evident that it was written and illuminated at the commencement of the fourteenth century. In the beginning of the book, is a great variety of washed drawings; the subjects of which are taken from the Old Testament; these are followed by the portraitures of several Saints; beautifully painted and decorated with gold; then succeeds a calendar, the psalter, with penitential hymns, and the litany; divided into seven parts; the whole enriched with finished paintings, and ornamented letters of gold, equal, if not superior, in point of workmanship, to any thing I ever saw in any MS of that æra. The drawings from which the twelve following plates are engraved, occur in the psalter, at the bottom of the leaves; a drawing of this kind belonging to every page. I have selected all that relate to the English History; but a great variety of other subjects are therein depicted; such as the miracles attributed to the Blessed Virgin; the martyrdom of several Saints mentioned in the golden legend; grotesque figures, and the like.

This superb manuscript formerly belonged to Queen Mary, and was presented to her in the year 1553, by Baldwin Smith, a citizen of London, as appears by an entry made in the last page. The press mark is 2 B. VII.

SUPPLEMENT

TO THE

Antiquities, Manners, Customs, &c.

of the ENGLISH.

PLATE I.

NUMBER I. IN the first compartment of this plate is represented St. Ursula, with her virgin companions, on ship board.

NUMBER II. In the second compartment, is delineated their martyrdom. The outlines of this fable, as it stands recorded in the golden legend, are as follow: A certain British king, whose name was Natus, or Mautus, had a daughter called Ursula; she was a young lady of extraordinary beauty, and as virtuous as she was fair. The king who at that time reigned in England, having heard of her perfections, demanded her in marriage of her father. Natus received the embassy with great marks of sorrow, because the English monarch was a Pagan: however, at length he consented to the union upon these conditions: Namely, That the king of England should renounce paganism and be baptized; that he should send eleven thousand virgins, save one, to accompany Ursula to the English court; and that she should be allowed the space of one year to prepare herself for the nuptials, during which time the Pagan prince might have leisure to be fully instructed in the principles of Christianity. It appears that these conditions were com-

B   plied

plied with, and the virgins accordingly were sent to the court of Natus. Ursula persuaded all these ladies to embrace the Christian faith, and when they went on ship board together, they wandered about the sea coasts to Rome, and several other places; but touching on their return at a port which belonged to a heathenish and barbarous people, they all suffered martyrdom, rather than renounce their belief in Christ.

This preposterous fable Mr. Casley, in his preface to the Catalogue of the Royal MSS. imagines to have originated entirely from a mistake in transcribing the Calender. "Upon seeing," (says he,) "in the twelfth of the " calends of November *Undecimille Virgo et Martyr*, some blunderer read " *Undecim mille*; and of course the words following must be changed into " *Virgines et Martyres*, and so has raised the story of eleven thousand Virgins " and Martyrs. *Undecimilla* a diminutive of *Undecima* was a woman's name, " because I suppose she was the eleventh child of her parents."

NUMBER III. In the third compartment is represented the martyrdom of St. Alban. The illuminator has, but I believe without any good authority, placed the regal crown upon the head of this Saint; the general opinion is, that he was a Roman by birth, and a person of some distinction. According to an old MS. which I have in my own possession, he was beheaded the 10th of July, A. D. 286, and with this account Bede also agrees, who informs us, that the martyrdom of St. Alban happened during the persecution of the Christians under Dioclesian.

In the first Volume of *The Manners and Customs of the English*, the reader will find among the delineations copied from a MS. of Mathew Paris, the miraculous manner in which the bones of this Saint were found by Ossa, king of Mercia, who erected a stately abbey at Verulum, now called St. Alban's, in honor of him.

PLATE II.

NUMBER I. THE first compartment of this plate represents the Condemnation of Edmund king of the East Angles. The personage seated upon the throne, with a crown upon his head, is Hinguar the son of Lodbroc the Dane. Lodbroc, according to some authors, came accidentally into Norfolk, and was entertained by Edmund. His expertness in hawking excited the jealousy of Bern, falconer to the king, and he slew him. The murder being discovered, Bern was banished from England, and going into Denmark, met with Hinguar the son of Lodbroc, to whom he mentioned the death of his father, but declared that he was slain by the express command of Edmund. Hinguar came with a large company of Danes into England, in order to revenge the murder of his father; and having secured the person of King Edmund, condemned him to be shot to death with arrows. Other authors, who admit not of the truth of this story, which indeed in its various circumstances favors too much of romance, attribute the death of this king, to his pious, and unshaken adherence to the Christian religion; and this opinion seems to be justified by his subsequent canonization, and by the great honors which were afterwards paid to his memory.

NUMBER II. In the second compartment is drawn the death of king Edmund, which, according to the abovementioned MS. in my own possession, happened on the twelfth day of December, in the year of our Lord 870. His body was first privately buried; but being afterwards discovered in a miraculous manner, was re-interred with great solemnity at Bury, in Suffolk, where an Abbey was erected and dedicated to him.

NUMBER III. The third compartment contains a representation of the ancient mode of administering the Sacrament of the Lord's Supper. This curious delineation does not appear to require any further explanation.

This plate, if placed in proper order, should follow the two succeeding ones, but as St. Alban and St. Edmund appear to have actually suffered in the defence of Christianity, and to have had an Abbey built in honor of each of them, I classed them as near together as the nature of the work would admit of.

PLATE III.

NUMBER I. IN the upper compartment of this plate Oswald king of Northumberland is represented with his army, proceeding against the king of Mercia, who had invaded his dominions.

All our historians agree that Oswald was a man of much piety, and of an amiable disposition. By his valour he united the kingdoms of Bernicia, and Deira, and made himself sole monarch over all the Northumbers. The glory he acquired by his martial conduct, as well as the great accession of power, which was the result of his conquests, excited the envy and jealousy of Penda, king of Mercia, a man whose restless and ferocious disposition rendered him capable of undertaking the most daring enterprises. Without any previous information, or regular declaration of war, he entered the dominions of Oswald, at the head of a large army, and ravaged the country with fire and sword whereever he came. Oswald collected all the forces together that he could upon so sudden an emergency, and both armies met at a place called Maserfield, in Shropshire, where, after a long and bloody conflict, the Northumbers were totally routed, and Oswald himself slain. This battle was fought on the fifth day of August, A.D. 642.

NUMBER II. The second compartment contains a delineation of the Battle at Maserfield, and Oswald is represented as falling from his horse, wounded by the Mercian king. Numberless are the miracles which have been attributed to Oswald after his death, and Bede informs us, that in his time the right hand of that unfortunate prince was preserved in the Church of Petersborough; concerning which the Monkish writers have related this story:—One day while he was sitting at dinner, he sent from his own table, a large silver dish full of meat, with orders that it should be given to the poor, and the dish itself broken into pieces and divided amongst them; upon which Aidan, one of the Roman missionaries who was present, took the king by the right hand, and said, " *May this hand never perish.*"

NUMBER

NUMBER III. In the bottom compartment of this plate is delineated one of the fabulous miracles attributed to the Virgin Mary. The resuscitated corps of a warrior appears rising from the tomb, to whom she presents a coat of mail, an angel attends upon her with a spear and an helmet. For the sake of these martial implements, especially the coat, or shirt, of mail, I was induced to engrave the delineation.

PLATE IV.

NUMBER I. THE delineation copied in the top compartment of this plate represents Cenelm, king of Mercia, with his attendants, hunting.

Cenelm was very young when he succeeded Cenwulf in the kingdom of Mercia. All our historians I believe agree, that his death was premature, though they differ widely with respect to the cause of it, whether it was by accident or design. Malmsbury, who inclines to the former opinion, concisely informs us, that his sister Quendreda, without any malicious intention, was the innocent occasion of his death; but the particulars of the accident are not related. On the other hand, the more modern writers accuse Quendreda either of slaying him herself, or causing him to be slain, in order to facilitate her own ascent to the throne of Mercia. They tell us in general, that he was assassinated while he was hunting; and that after the murder was committed, his body was secretly buried in or near the place where he was slain; and with this opinion our illuminator evidently agreed. The MS. which I have mentioned before, says that he was murdered on the 16th of August, A. D. 819.

NUMBER II. In the second compartment, the Regicides are represented in the act of throwing the dead body of the king into a pit. The monkish writers, who are always fond of the miraculous, have upon this occasion invented a very ridiculous story of a bird, which carried an inscription to Rome, by means of which the place was discovered were the corps of the unfortunate prince had been secreted; from whence it was taken and buried with great solemnity in the church of Winchomb, in Glocestershire.

NUMBER III. The delineation contained in the bottom compartment of this plate does not refer to any particular history, it is given to show the ancient habits of the Abbess, the Nun, and the Anchorite. The building behind

behind the Anchorite is intended by the delineator to represent the cell, or hermitage, in which he made his residence;—from the slightness of the drawing but little judgment can be formed concerning the materials of which this little structure consisted.

PLATE V.

NUMBER I. THE Royal Personage represented in the upper compartment of this plate with his attendants hunting, is Edward, sirnamed the Martyr.

NUMBER II. In the second compartment is delineated the manner in which that unfortunate prince was basely assassinated. The illuminator has attended very closely to the historical account of this infamous transaction; the principal circumstances of which are as follow: The young monarch being hunting in the Isle of Purbeck, as he pursued the game through a wood he passed near to Corfe Castle, the habitation of his step-mother Ælfrida, and willing to pay his respects to her, called at the gate of the castle: When it was made known that the king waited to see her she came out to him and entreated him to alight; but being intent upon his sport, he would not comply with her request, and only begged that a cup of wine might be brought to slake his thirst. The servant who presented the cup to him, being before-hand instructed by his mistress, stabbed him with a sword while he was drinking. The king, finding himself wounded, clapped his spurs to the horse, and endeavoured to make his escape; but fainting with the loss of blood, he fell from the saddle, and one of his feet being intangled in the stirrup, he was dragged up and down for a considerable time, and at last left dead in the wood. According to the MS. in my possession, which I have quoted before, this murder was committed on the 15th day of April, A. D. 978. The corps was first privately buried at Warham; but three years afterwards it was taken from thence, and re-interred with great pomp and solemnity at Shaftsbury.

Ælfrida was instigated to perpetrate this inhuman action, by the ambitious desire which she had entertained of seating her own son Æthelred upon the throne of England.

NUMBER III. The delineation copied in the lower compartment of this plate, and all of them contained in the seven plates which follow, relate to the life and transactions Thomas of Becket, whose history and character are so generally known, that no more will I presume be deemed necessary in the present publication, than a concise account of the subjects, in the order that they stand, without filling up the intermediate spaces of time, for which the reader must be referred to the histories of this country; or particularly to the Life of Henry the Second, by Lord Littleton, where, in the second volume, he will meet with ample satisfaction.

Becket's father, who is represented in this delineation, is said to have been a citizen of London, and was probably a merchant. Brompton informs us that his baptismal name was Gilbert, and that he lived on the spot where St. Thomas's Hospital now stands. It is generally agreed that Gilbert's wife was a foreigner, and according to some authors a native of Syria; conformable to this idea, our illuminator, in the present design, has drawn the lady departing from her relations, who are depicted cross-legged, and seated upon the ground, agreeable to the custom of the Eastern countries; but Brompton says that she was the daughter of a Saracen, who had taken Gilbert Becket prisoner as he went on a pilgrimage* to the Holy Land.

VI

PLATE VI.

GILBERT BECKET having brought the lady who had committed herself to his protection, into his native country, prevailed upon her to embrace the doctrines of Christianity, and caused her to be baptized previous to their marriage.

NUMBER I. The Baptismal Ceremony is represented in the upper compartment of this plate. From the circumstance of two bishops attending upon this occasion and the solemn manner in which the ceremony appears to be performed, we may safely conclude, that the illuminator did by no means agree with the more modern authors concerning the extreme indigence of Gilbert Becket, but rather that he thought directly contrary to them. Brompton tells us that he had been sheriff of London, and from the same writer we learn, that the Christian name of Becket's lady was Matilda; but on what authority he speaks I do not pretend to determine.

NUMBER II. In the middle compartment is delineated the solemnization of the nuptials between Gilbert Becket and his lady.

NUMBER III. In the third compartment we see represented Thomas Becket, soon after his birth, wrapped in swaddling cloths, and laid in a cradle by the side of his mother's bed.

In all of the ancient delineations which have fallen under my observation, representing the baptism of adults, I have constantly remarked, that the person baptised is drawn naked, or covered with a dress made to fit close to every part of the body, which from the size of the font, we may conceive to be half immerged in the water. In some marginal drawings of much earlier date than the present, I have found that a large vessel like a bathing tub is substituted for the font; a remarkable one of this kind occurs in a MS. in the

the Royal Library, at the British Museum, marked 13. E. VI. over which is written in Latin, " *Lucius, the first king baptized in England.*"

I do not see that there is any appearance of a ring used in the marriage ceremony of Becket and his Lady.

As these drawings are very neatly, and without doubt accurately executed, the reader will, I trust, examine with much pleasure the difference of manners, in the course of four or five centuries.

PLATE VII.

NUMBER I. ALL the intermediate circumstances relative to the life and transactions of Thomas Becket, from infancy to manhood, are passed over by our illuminator; and in the upper compartment of this plate he is represented receiving from king Henry the second, a letter sealed with the royal signet, constituting him Chancellor of England. Becket is said to have supported the office with great ostentation and profuseness; but as he appeared to have been perfectly devoted to the service of his sovereign, the king in return, took every opportunity of advancing his fortune.

NUMBER II. In the year of our Lord 1163 he was promoted to the See of Canterbury, and the solemnity of his consecration is depicted in the middle compartment of this plate. Having attained to that exalted dignity, as if he had nothing left to hope for from the favour of his Royal master, he threw off all appearance of respect and compliance; and was afterwards as resolute in his opposition to the will of the king, as he had been obsequious in obeying it before. The king, on the other hand, incensed by the ungrateful behaviour of the archbishop, withdrew his protection, and from a friend became a bitter enemy. Violent disputes were fomented between them, which were supported with unequalled pride and obstinacy on the part of Becket, who could not be prevailed upon, either by intreaties, or by threatenings, to comply with the king's command, which upon all occasions he set at defiance.

NUMBER III. But perhaps the haughty and overbearing disposition of the prelate was in no instance more forcibly manifested than in his refusing to

obey

obey the summons when cited to appear and answer to the charges alledged against him by the king. He afterwards presumed to approach the royal presence, holding the cross in his own hand, and habited in the pontifical robes of his office, and there openly expressed his disapprobation of the king's conduct, which transaction is very spiritedly represented in the lower compartment of this plate.

VIII

PLATE VIII.

THE daring and unprecedented step which Becket had taken in appearing at court, in the insolent manner before mentioned, so highly incensed the king, that he caused judgment to be instantly pronounced against him. In consequence of which he was apprehended as a traitor; but having by some means extricated himself from the hands of those who had taken him into custody, he fled without delay, secretly, to Sandwich, under the covert of a borrowed name, and embarked for Flanders, having first made his appeal to the See of Rome.

NUMBER I. In the delineation contained in the top compartment of this plate the Metropolitan is represented on ship-board, proceeding towards Flanders.

When the king heard of the departure, or rather flight, of Becket from England, and that he had appealed to the Pope; he was incensed to the greatest degree. Not satisfied with seizing upon his possessions, to his own use, he extended his resentment to the relations of the haughty prelate, causing all of them to be banished, not even excepting women and young children.

NUMBER II. The above circumstance is particularly attended to by our illuminator, and in the middle compartment of this plate, the king is represented denouncing, himself, the severe sentence. The manner in which the unfortunate relatives of Becket are prepared for their journey is well worthy of observation. I cannot properly ascertain the rank of that officer who stands at the king's left hand, bearing a mace upon his shoulder, and holding in his right hand a glove. The figure seated immediately behind the

king,

king, in the lower compartment of plate VII. is undoubtedly intended for the same person; as the countenance, and the cap which he wears appear to me sufficiently to testify, notwithstanding he is there drawn without the mace.

NUMBER III. In the bottom compartment of this plate, the relations of Becket, are represented in a ship, upon the sea, following him into Flanders.

PLATE IX.

NUMBER I. THE delineation copied in the top compartment of this plate represents the banished relations of Becket, after they were landed in Flanders, journeying in search of him.

NUMBER II. The interview between the archbishop and his friends, is delineated in the middle compartment of this plate. They informed him of the rigourous sentence which had been pronounced against them, by the king, made known their wants, and implored his protection. There is great expression of anger in the action and countenance of the proud prelate, as he is drawn by the illuminator. Becket it seems complained very bitterly, against the injustice of the king's conduct; but it does not appear that he was able to afford assistance, of any great extent, to his suffering relatives; for he himself declares, in his letter to the Pope, that those unfortunate dependants were reduced to very great hardships.

NUMBER III. The bottom compartment contains the Archbishop's interview with the Pope, when he took the ring from his finger and presented it to his holiness: this action was considered as a formal resignation of his See into the hands of the Roman Pontiff. Not only the king, but the generality of the clergy of England were offended at Becket's submission to the Pope, which they considered as a precedent of a very dangerous import; and it was the occasion of many serious disputes, between the party who supported the prerogative of the king, and the favourers of the Archbishop. Becket himself was not behind hand in fomenting these discords, seeking every opportunity he could to oppose the determinations of the king, and to stir up the minds of his subjects against him.

There could be no doubt but that the submission of Becket to the Pope would effectually ensure his protection. His Holiness returned to the Archbishop the insignia of his office, and confirmed him in his dignity. His power, however, did not extend so far as to restore him to his See; his menaces were despised by the king, who considered Becket as an insolent traitor.

PLATE X.

NUMBER I. THE delineation copied in the upper compartment of this plate, represents the Archbishop, in the habit of his office, seated at the Pope's right hand; the table is covered before them, and in the front a servant is kneeling and tasting the wine, previous to his offering it to the Pontiff or his guests. This design, the illuminator, I apprehend, has given in order to show how highly the English prelate stood in favour with his holiness.

NUMBER II. The Pope finding that he could not prevail upon the king of England to restore Becket to his See, and that a reconciliation between them did not seem likely to take place very suddenly, thought proper, till something more permanent could be done for him, to recommend him to the protection of the Abbot of Pontigni, a religious house in Burgundy: This circumstance claimed the illuminator's attention, and accordingly, in the middle compartment, we see represented, the Abbot, with his fraternity, in a very friendly manner, receiving the Archbishop on his arrival at Pontigni.

After long altercations, through the intercession of the king of France, and the partisans of Becket, king Henry was prevailed upon to consent to a second interview with the Archbishop. A former interview had taken place, which is not noticed by our illuminator, but through the sullen obstinacy of Becket, was not productive of any good effect.

Previous to his meeting with the king, Becket, in order to prepare himself for his *spiritual combat*, as it is called, went from the Abbey of Pontigni to a church at Soissons, to visit the sepulchre of Saint Drausius; and it is said that he watched all night before the shrine of that Saint. He watched also

also a second night before the shrine of Gregory the Great, whom he considered as the founder of the English church; and a third night before the altar of the blessed Virgin, whom he regarded as his patroness.

NUMBER III. The delineation copied in the lower compartment of this plate, without doubt refers to one of the above-mentioned Vigils; but to which of them it is most strictly applicable, I am at a loss to determine.

XI

PLATE XI.

NUMBER I. IN the upper compartment of this plate is delineated the interview between the king and Becket: They are represented taking each other's hand, in token of their being reconciled. The illuminator has well expressed the reluctance with which this show of friendship was performed. From the subsequent behaviour of both parties, it is evident that a hearty reconcilement was by no means the effect of the meeting; however, it seems to have answered the present purpose of both, to disguise their real sentiments upon this occasion.

NUMBER II. In consequence of the apparent reconciliation, Becket was restored to his See, and is accordingly represented, in the middle compartment of this plate, returning to England. He had not been long reinstated in his former power, before his proud and revengeful spirit manifested itself in several instances; and he still continued to act upon the same arbitrary principles as had occasioned his disgrace.

The king, who remained abroad, was continually hearing complaints against the conduct of Becket; and we may reasonably suppose, that his dislike of him was not lessened by them. Our historians inform us, that one day, as the king was sitting at dinner, some fresh instance of Becket's insolence being mentioned, he lamented that he had no faithful servant who would free him from so turbulent an enemy. This intimation of what he desired, fell not unnoticed to the ground; four knights, who attended at the court, entered into a confederacy together to destroy the Archbishop, and followed him into England to effect their purpose: Their design was not kept so secret, but that information of it reached the ears of Becket, who was several times warned to beware of them.

NUMBER III. The illuminator has attended to the circumstance before mentioned, and in the lower compartment of the present plate, we see the Archbishop seated at table, in his apartments at Canterbury; and a messenger is represented upon his knees before him, giving him information, that the four knights, his avowed enemies, had armed themselves, and only waited for an opportunity to destroy him; but, with his usual obstinacy, he neglected the salutary advice of his friends, resolving to enter the church as usual, and perform in person the duties of his function.

XII

PLATE XII.

NUMBER I. IN the top compartment of this plate is delineated the death of Becket. The four knights, whose names were, William de Tracy, Hugh de Morville, Richard Britton, and Reginald Fitzurse, entered the church, completely armed, and having found the Archbishop officiating at the high altar, after some short altercation, slew him there. This murder was committed with aggravated circumstances of brutal inhumanity; such as cutting off a part from his skull, and casting the brains about upon the pavement of the church. Becket was slain in the beginning of January, A. D. 1171.

The king, when he heard of the murder of Becket, expressed great sorrow, and abjured his having been intentionally concerned in it. By way of penance, some time after, he walked bare-footed to the tomb of that unfortunate prelate, where he submitted, voluntarily, to the ecclesiastic scourge.

NUMBER II. The burial of Becket is represented in the middle compartment of this plate.

NUMBER III. In the third compartment, the illuminator, who was probably himself an ecclesiastic, in order the better to justify his hero's claim to the title of a Saint, has depicted his reception into Paradise. The Spirit of the Prelate, supported by two Angels, is introduced to our blessed Redeemer, before whom he kneels, with great humility, holding his mitre in his left hand.

Innumerable are the miracles attributed to this Saint after his death; and the shrine, wherein his corps was contained, for beauty and riches, was scarcely to be equalled. The following description of it, taken from Dart's History of Canterbury Cathedral, may not, perhaps, be thought improper

in

in this place: "It was built," says he, "about a man's height, all of stone, then upward of timber, plain; within which was a chest of iron, containing the bones of Thomas Becket, skull and all, with the wound of his death, and the piece of his skull laid in the same wound. The timber work of this shrine on the outside, was covered with plates of gold, damasked and imbossed with wires of gold, garnished with broches, images, angels, chains, precious stones, and great orient pearls." Erasmus thus describes it: "They drew up with cords, a chest or case of wood, and then there was seen a chest or coffin of gold, and inestimable riches. Gold was the meanest thing that was there. It shone all over, and sparkled and glittered with jewels, which were very rare and precious, and of an extraordinary size: Some of them were bigger than a goose's egg. The Prior took a white wand, and touched every jewel, telling what it was, the French name, the value, and the donor of it; for the chief of them were gifts of monarchs." Thus far Erasmus: "Soon after which the shrine was demolished, the treasures of it seized to the king's use; which filled two great chests, which six or eight men could scarcely convey out of the church, and at the same time his bones were taken out and burned upon the pavement of the said church."

www.ingramcontent.com/pod-product-compliance
Lightning Source LLC
Chambersburg PA
CBHW031328230426
43670CB00006B/269